RESET

DWAIN SCHENCK

RESET

How to BEAT THE JOB-LOSS BLUES and Get Ready for YOUR NEXT ACT

Foreword by **Mika Brzezinski**,
New York Times bestselling author of
KNOWING YOUR VALUE

With insight and inspiration from:

MIKA BRZEZINSKI, DONALD TRUMP, CHRISTIE HEFNER,
MORT ZUCKERMAN, SUSIE ESSMAN, DONNY DEUTSCH,
LARRY DAVID, JOE ECHEVARRIA, MIKE BARNICLE,
JOE SCARBOROUGH

Da Capo

LIFE
LONG

A Member of the Perseus Books Group

Book designed by Cynthia Young
Set in 12 point Adobe Garamond Pro

**Cataloging-in-Publication data for this book
is available from the Library of Congress.**
First Da Capo Press edition 2014
ISBN 978-0-7382-1695-9 (paperback)
ISBN 978-0-7382-1696-6 (e-book)

Published by Da Capo Press
A Member of the Perseus Books Group
www.dacapopress.com

Da Capo Press books are available at special discounts for bulk purchases in the U.S. by corporations, institutions, and other organizations. For more information, please contact the Special Markets Department at the Perseus Books Group, 2300 Chestnut Street, Suite 200, Philadelphia, PA, 19103, or call (800) 810-4145, ext. 5000, or e-mail special.markets@perseusbooks.com.

10 9 8 7 6 5 4 3 2 1

◇

Dedicated to
Jack, Nicola and Natalie,
whom I love equally with all my heart

Unemployment is a tragedy dressed in a clown suit.

CONTENTS

ACKNOWLEDGMENTS

Reset would not have seen the light of day without the love and support of my close friend Mika Brzezinski. The recession was roaring full-force and I was out of work. "Write about it," she said. She told me how it would help thousands of people keep their sanity through the worst job market since the Great Depression. She said it would help me along the way as well. She was right. Mika, you're the sister I never had.

This book would have hit a dead end if it weren't for the extraordinary men and women who shared their insights and advice with me. This is their reality and therefore their book too. Their stories and inspiration are timeless no matter the jobs numbers or economic climate. Nobody writes a book without a great deal of behind the scenes help, and I would be remiss in not thanking Mika's *Morning Joe* co-host, the indefatigable Joe Scarborough, for his support throughout this journey and writing what he called, "an important story in our life and times we live in."

Sincere and everlasting thanks are due my friend Mark Samuels who kept me sane throughout this labor of love that at times was more *labor* than love. Thank you for pushing me when I waivered. Thank you to my longtime friend, colleague and veteran writer/adventurer/PR man extraordinaire, Jeff Blumenfeld, who challenged me to write *a* book in the first place. Your counsel was invaluable. To Phil Cannon, who most importantly makes me laugh and whose guidance kept me on course every step of the way. Jeff Pennington, thanks for always being there for me—since the sixth grade. You are like blood to me.

To my editor Dan Ambrosio and all the talented people at Da Capo Press; thank you for your deft touch and eternal cheerfulness. Thank you to David Steinberger for saying yes to what I had to say. With all my admiration I thank my special friend Paul Stuhlman for his help throughout this project. He is truly a gift to anyone looking for a job. I have been inspired on nearly a daily basis by this professional who devotes his life to helping others find a job and keep their sanity.

My love goes out to my parents who have always been there for me and my family—especially through the lean times that this book addresses. Love to my Aunt Sharon who is special in so many ways, too numerous to count. For my in-laws, Gene and Theresa; I am enormously grateful for your support and understanding. Congratulations to my brother for staying the course and landing so successfully—before he even had this book to use as a blueprint.

And finally, my deepest gratitude and appreciation goes to my wife for the grace and happiness she brings to our family each and every day. I owe her the most thanks of all. Thank you for always being by my side and often times leading the way. Our children are truly blessed to have you as their mother.

FOREWORD BY
MIKA BRZEZINSKI

We all have friends who seem to have figured it out early on and become successful, *solid* and stable in their lives and careers. Dwain and Colleen were those friends to me, the solid ones who have it all, right away, and keep it, seemingly forever—the perfect house and the nice cars. Colleen is beautiful, a cross between Julia Louis-Dreyfus and Andie MacDowell—very grounded—and that made me want to be like her. But it was an unattainable goal.

It was still early in my career, and I was working for the overnight *Up to the Minute* news program at CBS network news. I was struggling to climb the ranks, and I started to think I would never attain a salaried position that would keep me afloat. I was always scrambling to pay my bills.

In the meantime, Dwain had transitioned flawlessly from working as a TV reporter at a cable news station to head up public relations for one of the country's largest disaster relief agencies. Their biggest struggle was whether Colleen should give up her great position at Deloitte & Touche to be a stay-at-home mom with their new baby boy. I was envious. They were that solid, because they had those choices and were lucky enough to be in *that* comfortable place.

I couldn't get it together; the hours I was working were killing me. I wasn't sleeping as a result of my ridiculous schedule, and when I could steal away for a few hours of rest I was unable to set my mind at ease. I wanted my children to grow up and be proud of their mother. I wanted my colleagues and bosses to see what a hard worker I was, and I wanted to be a great wife. I wanted to do it all, but it always felt just out of reach for me. Not for Dwain and Colleen. They had cracked the code.

Don't get me wrong. I loved socializing with them. We always had a blast at dinner. But I was always left asking myself, "What am I doing wrong?" I couldn't help thinking how good they were compared to me.

In March of 2012 my husband and I made plans to meet them for a long-overdue dinner like we had always done over the years. I had bounced back from a year of unemployment after being fired as a news anchor and *60 Minutes* correspondent at CBS to become cohost on MSNBC's highly rated morning program *Morning Joe*. Unemployment had battered my spirit, but it hadn't won the war over my will to work.

It was a whole new world. Job growth in our country was paltry, and we were living through the most substantial economic downturn since the Great Depression. To put it in perspective, the median family net worth dropped a staggering 40 percent, and we were still recovering at a snail's pace from a recession brought on by the collapse of the housing bubble that sucked an astonishing $7.38 *trillion* out of the economy.

Despite all the bad news, I was on top of the world as a result of my new job! I was excited that for once I would feel that I had my act together in front of the very people whose position had seemed so unattainable.

Shortly after the hugs and small talk, we learned that the tables had turned in a terrible and most unexpected way. Over the course of the meal, Dwain told us how he had become a casualty of the

Great Recession—not once, but twice, having lost a ten-year-old business in 2009, rebounded, and then lost another job with a Fortune 500 company in 2012. He had joined the more than twenty million people who had suddenly lost their jobs, many by no fault of their own.

I was blown away by this reversal of fortune. Here were my solid friends, who in my mind were always going to be okay, and suddenly their life had cracked open. A tsunami hit our economy, and millions of highly educated upper-middle-class workers—a majority of whom were middle-aged men—were out of work. Still . . . Dwain??

We had met Dwain more than twenty years ago when I was just starting my career in news at the FOX affiliate in Hartford, Connecticut. He was one of the best PR guys I had ever met. He was easy to talk to, intelligent, understood what news people like me needed, and could write a great press release. His reputation shot up in the industry like a rocket and stayed in orbit for decades.

He went on to work for several corporations before starting his own boutique PR agency, where he provided services to iconic brands and high-profile individuals such as the governor of Connecticut, Dannel P. Malloy, and the Kennedy-Skakel family.

Over dinner, Dwain described the dehumanizing impact unemployment was having on him over time. His stories cut to my core. Without hesitation my advice that night was, "You need to write about this. You can help people." I truly believed a book like this could help millions learn how to avoid or at least reduce some of the psychological trauma associated with joblessness, which is right up there with the trauma of losing a loved one or divorce.

I knew firsthand the hopelessness and anxiety that goes with unemployment. There were weeks I couldn't muster the energy to look for a job. It was the most frustrating, difficult, and debilitating time of my life. As my husband and I sat listening to Dwain, I realized how long I had put my life, my friendships, and my sense of self-worth on hold. I had closed myself off from the world, not even knowing what had happened to one of my best friends. He was now in the same boat I had been in, and I felt like I was drowning all over again just thinking about his struggle.

His marriage, his family, his friends, his whole sense of being had been turned inside out, and I knew exactly how he was feeling because I had gone through it too. I shut myself off to the world and my family. I was flailing and searching for answers to how to deal with my emotional state and how to simply go about landing a job.

He talked about the loss of identity and the messiness of being unemployed. He was articulate about his feelings and what he was doing to regain and maintain his spirit. I thought, *Where was he when I was unemployed!?* Like him, I hated being that little speck—that tiny, tiny tip of the needle—so small and thinking no one, absolutely not a soul, knows I'm out here.

Dwain has finally written *our* story, perhaps your story and a loved one's story, because that one word, *unemployed,* affects us all. This is an outstanding book that speaks about the real world today, what happened in the past, and how there are plenty of brighter tomorrows that lie ahead. It is also entertaining and practical to the core.

It beautifully captures his thoughts, advice, and inspirations surrounding his journey into the abyss of unemployment and the inner struggle waged when you can't find a job. Whether deconstructing the *business* of becoming gainfully employed or offering advice and commentary from colorful characters along the way, from everyday people to experts, celebrities, and business leaders from a wide range of industries, he talks about how to survive this sometime modern apocalypse—and even thrive.

From life-altering identity crises, he shows us how to keep our head even if our world is seemingly crumbling down on every level. This story is for those who *never* thought they would be unemployed—who *shouldn't* be—and how not to feel alone, when you essentially are!

You will come to realize that being unemployed has its value too. I am better on television today than I ever would have been if I hadn't lost my job. As a person, as a mother, as a wife, and as a professional, the best thing that ever happened to me was being unemployed. You only discover that after passing through it.

Unemployment shows you what you're made of. You are starting all over again, and that's just the way it goes. And if you have children, you are showing them the measure of a man or a woman—that you have the guts to start over and do whatever it takes to make it back—whether that means landing a new job, changing careers, retiring, or perhaps starting your own business.

What do you have to offer? That's what everyone in this new economy has to figure out. That's what I asked of Dwain when he had nothing, and he has taken us on a fascinating journey of self-discovery and redefined what *solid* means to me today.

Reset: How to Beat the Job Loss Blues and Get Ready for Your Next Act soars to the heavens. I applaud Dwain for his work and his desire to help all of us see how bright our future can be.

Mika Brzezinski
Cohost of MSNBC's *Morning Joe* and
best-selling author of *Knowing Your Value*

INTRODUCTION

Layoff. If you haven't experienced one, you know someone who has. I speak with authority: not only have I seen energetic, talented, and accomplished friends undergo the stress of job loss, but I too—no lightweight in the career department—have felt the sting of being "let go."

Much has been said—and written—about the changing work landscape, of the disappearing act of once-guaranteed pensions and employment-for-life business cultures. Welcome to the brave new world of job *in*security. I don't need to pound that drum further. Where I *can* shed light is on how we respond to layoffs: how we can beat the job-loss blues and get ready for our next act. Layoffs, position eliminations, departmental reorganizations, corporate moves and closures—whatever the boss or HR person calls it—are usually outside our control. But what we do *afterward* is firmly in our own hands.

Reset is the story of a journey. Of a successful journalist, businessman, and communications professional (me) who joined the ranks of the unemployed during one of the most dismal job markets in modern history. Of how my initial reactions (denial, depression) sabotaged my morale and motivation. And of how, with the assistance of friends, wisdom from experts, and good old-fashioned creativity and tenacity, I turned my attitude around. The hard-won, valuable advice and techniques in these pages can work for anyone concerned about job loss and can position you to get back on your feet and, with the right approach, land in a better place.

———

But back to the story of how this book began . . . with a layoff. Unemployment strikes deep into our psyche. Beyond the devastating loss of income, a layoff can shift our habits and lifestyle, unhinge our sense of self, and drive a wedge into a marriage.

I experienced all this and more the day I came home with my proverbial pink slip. My first reaction was to run away, emotionally and physically. My wife, Colleen, wanted to talk about it; I wanted to avoid the topic. Intellectually, I knew it was stupid to let something like unemployment get between us, but emotionally I felt like abandoning ship, isolating myself, just packing up and moving out. In the days and weeks that followed, things were no better. Gone were the mornings when I would get up with purpose, take the girls to school, then have a job to go to. My sense of identity was shot. The job loss was decimating our personal finances. Could I continue to keep a roof over my family's head, provide food to eat, new clothes to wear—would there be money left over to do fun things together? I came to realize that I had connected nearly my entire self-worth to my job title and to what I accomplished as a journalist and communications executive. Because I was no longer solving problems at work or collaborating as a valued team leader, I didn't feel like a productive member of society. My psyche was crushed.

Then I started to think about what was keeping me back. I wondered, *Is it possible that I'm not alone in these feelings and the befuddlement of what to do about it?* I realized I had hit a nerve when I described what I was going through to my friend Mika

Brzezinski, cohost of MSNBC's *Morning Joe*. She implored me to write this book and talk about the enormous emotional journey a person undergoes while looking for work, especially now, in one of the worst US job markets since the Great Depression.

She then told me about her own experience being unemployed, how she felt washed up and nearly convinced herself that she would never work again—this coming from a woman who had been an anchor at CBS network news and is now a best-selling author, coveted motivational speaker, and successful media force. Millions of people are going through similar situations but are just not talking about it, Mika pointed out, and many are desperate to validate feelings they've never experienced before, such as loneliness, worthlessness, and loss of purpose. What if I could figure out how to cope with these strong emotions and perhaps even harness them to help me go forward? What could relieve me of those nighttime panics where I would wake in a cold sweat worrying about the future and how I was going to pay the bills? As a journalist the only thing I could think to do was talk to others about it and ask questions. That was the only answer that made sense to me.

Mika was right; I was learning that the emotional side of unemployment is something few people discuss. This was true of many people I knew who were let go. They jumped feet first into the tactics of getting back in the workforce without setting up a strategy to deal with the emotional journey. The problem is, you can find yourself doing all the right things tactically but not making progress (and not understanding why) if you don't spend the time addressing what is knocking your self-esteem for a loop.

"The confidence problem is a big one, because that is usually the first thing that is shaken in a person," says Pamela Mitchell, one of the country's pre-eminent career reinvention experts and founder of the Reinvention Institute. "People think that the old way should work. They are doing it like they always have done it, and it no longer works. And they get frustrated."

No matter how you wound up out of work, it takes months for most people to register the enormity of the tectonic shift in their world. But in time it sinks in, and for many, short of terminal illness, they start to see how long-term unemployment can be the worst thing to happen to a person. It cuts you out of the herd like a pack of circling hyenas making breakfast out of a wildebeest calf on the grassy plains. You lose touch with colleagues and your workplace social network. The stress can lead to further terrible things happening in your life like divorce and suicide.

On May 2, 2013, the AP's Mike Stobbe reported that the suicide rate among middle-aged Americans went up 28 percent from 1999 to 2010, a period that by no coincidence included the recession and the mortgage crisis. The trend was most pronounced among middle-aged white men and women between thirty-five and sixty-five. Their suicide rate jumped a staggering 40 percent during that same decade.

Stobbe raises the question, "Why did so many middle-aged whites—that is, those who are 35 to 64 years old—take their own lives? One theory suggests the recession caused more emotional trauma in whites who tend not to have the same kind of church support and extended families that blacks and Hispanics do."

To me, coping with unemployment is similar to experiencing the five stages of grief laid out in the groundbreaking book *On Death and Dying* by Swiss American psychiatrist Elisabeth Kübler-Ross, a pioneer in near-death studies. As with coming to terms with our mortality, maybe coming to a new understanding and acceptance that this is the way the world is now will set us free and help us make adjustments to better deal with this economy.

After all, it's not a stretch to say we are talking about a crisis of almost biblical proportion. There's an economic term for people who have been out of work for more than a year and find themselves overlooked by companies as the economy, albeit somewhat shrunken, moves on without them: *hysteresis*. This is one of the worst by-products of a long recession, according to one of my favorite writers on the subject, Don Peck, in his book *Pinched: How the Great Recession Has Narrowed Our Futures and What We Can Do About It*. Hysteresis is the kiss of death for the rank-and-file unemployed, especially during a buyers' market when employers can be super picky and as job skills erode. Peck notes that in this situation, social networks shrink, references disappear, and employers, sensing personal and professional dysfunction, pass them over for more recently unemployed workers.

What can be done to prevent this? I didn't have to go far to find people willing to talk about it. Some were in the throes of lengthy unemployment, others had recently landed new jobs; they were all willing to open up about how they are managing the changing tides. I also talked with influential entrepreneurs and business leaders, including Christie Hefner, Donald Trump, Donny Deutsch, and the CEO of Deloitte LLP, Joe Echevarria. I spoke with media moguls like Mortimer B. Zuckerman, owner of the *New York Daily News*, and Arianna Huffington and entertainers like *Seinfeld* creator Larry David, as well as career coaches, respected executive recruiters, psychologists, and career reinvention experts. They generously shared their wisdom, advice, and stories about how they beat their job-loss blues and how they better prepared themselves for a second, third, or even fourth act.

Ultimately, I think the true value of this book boils down to one word: *perspective*. During an extended period of job loss, perspective flies out the window. What I have learned is that it's our *job* to make sure that doesn't happen.

An old friend used to say, "Time takes time." For some reason those three words resonate with me, slow me down, and help me take stock of what's going on around me and what's important. It's like a minimeditation. There are many reasons we become unemployed. Some are complicated and some are simple, but everybody has to work their way through them. Unemployment is a wake-up call, and what you choose to do with it is up to you. It's an opportunity to build yourself a much stronger foundation. In sharing my story, personal victories, and proven methods of finding work—along with ideas from the other brilliant contributors—you'll see that, no matter what happens, you can take yourself from point A to point Z—*and you will*. That sense of strength comes from your own self-determination and from a little faith. That is real power.

When the economy will turn around and happy times will return again is anybody's guess (for some, happy times never left). Many economists point to 2018 as the magic date. According Don Peck, "true recovery is not simply a matter of jolting the economy back onto its former path; it's about changing the path. Many of the deepest economic trends that the recession has highlighted and temporarily sped up will take decades to fully play out." Keep in mind that it took more than twenty-five years for the housing market to recover and the economy to right itself after the crash of 1929—that's about a generation.

I don't have a crystal ball to see the economic future either, but I can say this: those who start to think counterintuitively and learn to navigate these changing tides and address the emotional strain of unemployment will have fulfilling lives no matter where their career takes them. For that reason, this book isn't solely for the unemployed. It's for anyone who has a good job today, because you never know what tomorrow may bring. You must be prepared to hit your own reset button and come up with plan B as quickly and painlessly as possible.

AUTHOR'S NOTE

This book is based on my personal experience and on interviews I conducted. I've recorded it all as faithfully as possible, especially as I want my readers to find the information both credible and helpful. Because I was writing a book that includes stories of workplace trouble, job loss, and other personal difficulties, however, I decided to change a few names and identifying details. These minor changes were simply intended to protect the privacy of the people involved.

1

MY STORY

The Emotional Phases
of Unemployment

*H*ouston . . . *we have a problem.*

That was the first thought that crossed my mind when my boss summoned me to his office on the evening of March 19, 2012. I had been waiting for him to weigh in on changes to the weekly roundup newsletter I wrote. It was not unusual for him to put me off for hours even though he knew I was under a tight deadline.

My stomach filled with butterflies as I left my cubicle. Approaching his desk, I saw him looking at me with his signature blank stare. I instinctively knew this was the end. I crossed his office threshold and felt a fan of air against my back as an invisible hand shut the door behind me. The HR business leader took a seat next to me. I didn't take my eyes off her. As far as I was concerned, my boss wasn't in the room. I was furious and loathed his existence at this point.

My stomach was in knots. I had never been let go, but I knew plenty of people who had recently, in an economy where companies were slashing workers in record numbers, adding to the national unemployment rate that was hovering around 8.5 percent. The real numbers were much higher, more like 15 percent. It wasn't pretty.

So here I sat, in front of my boss, the third I had reported to in less than two years with the company. I was listening to the HR leader terminate me, but I wasn't hearing what she was saying. It reminded me of the *Peanuts* cartoons where adults speak in unintelligible honks: *wha, wha, whaan*. It had taken me a grueling yearlong search to land at this Fortune 500 company, and now I was being cast off during one of the worst job markets in a century. It was an outrage. In my mind this was a slow-motion catastrophe happening in fast-forward. It was clear that my boss was cleaning house to bring in his own team. He manufactured problems, manipulated the facts, and twisted reality to fit his story line. Never mind how unjust it was or how I had tried to head this day off for months by disputing these distortions with human resources. The bottom line: he wanted me out and had been building a case against me for months. I, however, wanted my job. I needed this job. I worked hard to get and keep the job, reinforced by earning stellar midyear employee reviews and the maximum bonus from my two previous supervisors. Now all I could do was sit there with a sock in my mouth and take the punishment.

The meeting concluded with my accepting a separation agreement in return for three months' severance and outplacement services. Not bad, I guess, for what turned out to be a fairly short-lived job. The HR leader handed over more documents to read and then followed me to my cubicle, where she robotically collected my computer, employee badge, and cell phone. I thought, *I'm now going to be accompanied out of the building by a couple of guys who look like they bounce for Hooters.* Instead, I was told I could leave the building without an escort as long as I did not stop and talk to anyone along the way. *Like I was going to broadcast the fact that I was no longer working at the company because my boss kicked me out.* I gathered up my notebook and other odds and ends. "We'll box up the rest of your stuff and mail it to you," the HR leader said in the most helpful voice she could muster.

How could a job that started out so well end so poorly? Less than two years earlier I had been hired as the new VP of communications for the US market for one of the world's most iconic brands. It was a huge break, putting an end to a job search that started when my own PR business was sputtering to stay alive after the recession put a stranglehold on the economy. By mid-2008 most of my clients had either gone out of business or, like my anchor clients, experienced drastic cutbacks; PR services were often the first thing to go.

I loved my new boss, the one who originally hired me, at my new gig. He was young, smart, and supportive. Three months after hiring me, though, he left the company for more responsibility and much more money. That caught me by surprise. I was disappointed and concerned that drastic change was afoot. Things worked out. I inherited his boss. She was a firecracker—smart and full of vitality—who had been with the company for a very long time and rose quickly through the ranks. She too was supportive and valued my skills and what I brought to her department.

I loved my job and looked forward to arriving early to get a jump on the day. I thought I was the luckiest guy in the world. I had a great job that paid decently during the worst economy in modern history, and I was starting to apply my skills and learn about a new industry. What more could you ask for?

Then my new, *new*, inherited boss got promoted.

Bam, it was the *World According to Garp* under boss number 3. Within a month he fired a colleague who had started a month before me. Number 3 was impossible to read, played the devil's advocate on every issue, and answered most questions *with a question*. You know the type. He was dour, pessimistic, and negative. He loved meetings. He was all strategy. He was the king of paralysis through analysis—the polar opposite of my first manager, which worried me. No, it put the fear of God into me is more like it. With boss number 3 it was all business while you were on the clock; when you weren't on the clock, you avoided him at all cost.

Two months into the job, he showed his true colors. Returning from a business trip where we had given a presentation to one of our biggest clients, he and I were standing in a busy train station with people going to and fro, literally bumping into each other on their way to their train platforms, when he sort of squared off and asked me in what seemed a hostile tone at the time, "Dwain, do you want my job?"

I was floored. What a loaded question! He was my third boss, and I was still getting to know him. I hadn't even been with the company for eighteen months, not to mention I was new to the industry and working hard to prove myself. It was absurd to think that I was gunning for his job, and I didn't feel qualified to even fill that role at this point.

What possessed him to ask that question in a crowded train station, of all places? It was so ill timed that I thought at first he was attempting to be humorous, which was also absurd, but at that point I was grasping at straws. I was a fish out of water with this guy. He liked it that way.

He was trying to intimidate me. How should I answer? Prior to asking me if I wanted his job, he had finished a five-minute-long critique of our meeting with the client. There were reasons the meeting went the way it did, and it was a successful meeting without the perceived barriers he was throwing up. He was frustrated that I didn't drive the meeting, but I was accompanying him as a new boss, and he knew all the players and had ten years' more industry experience than I did. I chose to try not to be perceived as attempting to show him up in the meeting. In some twisted way, did he perceive me to be a threat now because of it? Surely not.

I decided the best way to answer was to dance around the question and tell him I was busy with my current responsibilities. "I'm happy where I am," I said.

"So, you're happy treading water then?" he replied with a straight face. I thought to myself, *Is this for real?* It was offensive, but I kept my cool. Was he baiting me? What was he talking about, treading water? He was picking a fight. I took a deep breath. I needed to keep my emotions in check. He shot back, "So, where do you see yourself in a year?" We're in a train station in Delaware!

And so it went. Pure torture. Up was down, white was yellow, who's on first . . . anybody? Through all this, the guy had the balls to say he just had my best interests at heart. "Don't you believe me?" he would ask. No, I didn't believe him, but there wasn't anything I could do about it at the time, or ever for that matter.

● **SO, ON A BEAUTIFUL** March evening, I walked out of corporate headquarters with separation papers in hand and took a huge, deep breath. For the first time in months, I actually looked around and appreciated the sunset and beautifully manicured campus. Nonetheless, the situation was grave and daunting. I was aware that twenty million people were unemployed or underemployed and that a huge percentage of them were middle-aged, white-collar workers just like me.

I told myself not to worry; I was too good for this company anyway. I had a plan. An eerie sense of calm swept over me. Mika later warned me of this feeling. In a 2009 blog, she brilliantly articulated the emotions a person experiences after being let go: "Many 'friendships' from work evaporate, quickly, for all sorts of disappointing reasons. There is denial. Fake Bliss. (I am so glad I am out of there! I am, I really am. What a mess that place was!) Then reality—You can't stop asking why."

In my first weeks of unemployment, I was totally enveloped in that fake bliss she was referring to. It was intoxicating. *Everything will be fine*, I told myself. *I have a solid network of friends, and whether I liked it or not, it was time to move on. I'll have a job in less than a month this time around.*

I felt empowered with a sense of freedom I had not felt for years. In my mind, I was highly marketable. Because I had been working for nearly two years, I paid little attention to jobs numbers or the unemployment rate. I was pretty convinced that there were opportunities out there for me and that other companies would be looking for my unique skill set and knowledge.

On the drive home I called my wife on her cell to tell her the news. She didn't say much. She listened to me go on and on about how this was probably a *good* thing. Her silence led me to believe she was probably thinking to herself, *that's a crock of shit but keep telling yourself that.* I could tell she was more than concerned. I told her everything would be okay and that I already had several irons in the fire. Looking back, I realize my wife already knew the lunacy and sorrow I, *we*, would face with my being out of work, again, in this job market from hell. She knew deep down I was scared about the future and angry at how things had turned out.

Ironically, the cruel truth is I had played a role in hiring number 3. My second boss allowed me to interview him prior to making her decision. Although he lacked personality and the social skills of my other two bosses, it was undeniable that he stood out as the most qualified candidate. In the end, I hired my own executioner. It reminds me of a passage in one of my favorite novels by Abraham Verghese, *Cutting for Stone.*

> Life. . . . You live it forward, but understand it backward. It is only when you stop and look to the rear that you see the corpse caught under your wheel.

Today I was that corpse.

Layoff—It's a Family Affair

I pulled in the driveway prepared to tell Colleen all the reasons getting fired was good for us. I was planning to tell her that I'll find something that better fits my talents and temperament. I just needed a few minutes to convince her of that.

In reality, words failed me. I walked in the door, said hello, and hightailed it downstairs to my desk and computer in the basement.

I avoided eye contact. She needed eye contact. She wanted eye contact. I didn't have it to give. She needed reassurance that I was okay and that we would be okay. I wasn't so sure and she knew it.

Colleen bounded down the stairs after me and stood staring as I sat at my desk. She started to cry. I wasn't expecting that and snapped at her to stop. It made me uncomfortable to see her like this. *For God's sake, I haven't been out of work for more than an hour and she's already falling apart.* "Everything's going to be fine. This is no big deal. I'll be out of work three, four weeks tops. I've got a network of gold—you know I have friends I can call on to help me find a job."

I've been working in one way or another since I was a sophomore in high school, when my best buddy and I painted houses in the summer. I was always working and was proud of putting in a hard day's work. I worked my way through college, spending summers catching albacore tuna on a commercial fishing boat. After college I became an award-winning on-air television reporter and was wooed away from that job by the humanitarian relief agency AmeriCares. So naturally I'm thinking, *How long could it take me to land a new job?* The answer I chose to believe was, *Not long!* Unemployment was not a part of my ethos. Unemployment was incongruent to who I was. Yet here I sat—jobless.

Colleen looked at me, listening. She still hadn't voiced a word, but her face said it all. She was very worried. She later told me she was worried more about how this experience would wreak havoc on my self-worth than anything else. Looking back, I'm glad she didn't say that to me at the time, because I would have been clueless as to what she was talking about. This has nothing to do with my self-worth, I thought then.

Her emotions caused me distress. I was hovering on a high of fake bliss (thanks, Mika), a pink cloud, upbeat about the future, and Colleen was standing there crying. She was actually living in the real world this very day, both feet firmly planted on the basement floor. She finally walked over and put her arms out to me. We held each other, but I felt a million miles away when it came to trying to comfort her. I felt that I had been treated unjustly and now had three months to land a job before my severance ran out.

I tried to be sensitive to Colleen, but I was gearing up for a go-it-alone battle to find a job, and find it fast. I wasn't interested in processing sadness or other emotions surrounding what had just happened. Denial provided the protective armor I believed I'd need to land that other job as quickly as possible in today's hyper-competitive market.

Looking back, I see that my wife's emotions and concerns were spot-on. Always the optimist and realist—two great qualities—she recognized what we were in for long before I did. She knew that a forty-nine-year-old white guy looking for work in this market would find the going would be brutal. If I had a do-over, I would have been more sympathetic and listened to her advice, but in that defining moment I had made up my mind that this problem was mine, and solely mine, to work through and conquer. Once I land a job, I'd rejoin her and the family. Then life would continue as normal.

This attitude was the biggest mistake I made during my job search. Don't go it alone. Unemployment *is* a family affair—at the minimum an affair between spouses, partners, lovers, friends . . . anyone you care about or are close to. Unemployment turns the family structure inside out. It was insane not to lean on a wife as supportive as Colleen, but the fear was already setting in. I wanted to go it alone, but that's not practical when you have a family to care for. I had heard plenty of stories of out-of-work guys considering the opportunity to spend more time with the family a blessing. I love my family, but unemployment hasn't worked that way for me. Beneath the surface, our family was pushed to the brink. The kids struggled to cope with my ups and downs during the search, and marital sex nearly came to a standstill.

As the pink bliss of the newly laid-off began to fade, fear quickly started to eat at me. Some people find a moderate degree of fear a motivator; for me it only makes things worse. I never had trouble motivating myself to get things done. So now, this time of fear meant I wanted everything to stay the same in the house. I didn't want to cut back on services or let this setback affect our lifestyle one iota.

Colleen had other plans. She didn't panic, but she took a logical approach to the changes thrust upon us. We both agreed that we would try to keep the kids in the loop on what had happened to me. The kids knew that I would be home more and looking for a job. They also knew that they had been born to a father who was very type A to put it mildly, so adjustments would have to be made around the house. As best I could tell, they took my job loss in stride. They knew enough about what was going on in the country and had plenty of classmates whose fathers were out of work. I still sometimes felt like a loser around them. *Why isn't this fat bastard working instead of hanging out all day in the basement?* I would imagine one of my daughters thinking. Of course, that couldn't be further from the truth. I wasn't a complete bastard.

A couple of nights after my layoff, Colleen said she thought we needed to cut back our cable service. I laughed to myself. I knew she had been dying to drop some cable programming. This was the excuse she was looking for. She cut out HBO long ago, much to my consternation, even though we rarely watched it. She hated wasting money, even if it was only a whopping $7.35 per month. Yet, with echoes of her saying "every little bit helps" ricocheting in my head, it wasn't worth the fight.

Comedy Central was on the chopping block under Colleen's new savings plan. This was one of my son's favorite channels. For months we fought with him over two of its marquee shows, *Jackass* and *Tosh.0*. They were adult oriented and for the most part rude and inappropriate. The final straw was when I popped into the den, only to discover my eleven- and thirteen-year-old daughters and a friend watching an episode of *Jackass* where one character started barfing inside a space helmet—somehow induced by this very fat man farting into the wide part of a funnel that penetrated the helmet's face shield. The "astronaut" literally fell to his knees and threw up all over his own face. Stop. I'm not making this up. Who would produce programming like this?

I went ballistic. "Turn this crap off," I yelled. "Why are you watching this garbage?" My daughters were mortified by my outburst while their friend was visiting the house, but I blew a gasket. "That's it; I am getting rid of this now." I stormed out of the room and marched down the hall where I intercepted Colleen folding clothes in our older daughter's room.

"Colleen, do you know what the kids are watching?" I yelled. "Some guy on TV just pulled his pants down and shit into a tube attached to some guy's face. Why do you allow them to watch this bullshit?" When I finally took a breath and finished embarrassing the girls with my profanity-laced diatribe, Colleen calmly replied: "That is why I have asked you a hundred times to block the channel. This is why I am dropping cable."

Every little bit counts. *More could be saved here than money*, I thought just then.

Colleen also insisted that we cancel our trash collection service. The way she looked at it, I now had plenty of time between interviews to haul the garbage to the town dump for free. In these ways and others, she took a scalpel to our expenses, letting me focus 100 percent of my time looking for a new job. It seemed like a good plan.

Bring On the Interviews

Within a week of my termination, I had set up interviews with two reputable companies looking for senior-level communications people. The first company was looking for someone to head up public relations for its web portal in the news gathering field. The job was right up my alley, having started my career as a television reporter and studied journalism at the University of Southern California. This job would allow me to blend my two favorite vocations, journalism and PR, to help promote this site around the world. I was introduced to the CEO through a mutual contact, so I believed I would be interviewing with the decision maker. Looking back, I'm not sure that was the case. More on that later.

The interview went as well as I had hoped. Although I had not interviewed in quite some time, I considered my interviewing skills up to snuff. I arrived well prepared, having thoroughly researched the company and the job description. I thought I was the perfect fit for the position, but my Achilles' heel was my lack of digital publishing experience. When I say "lack" I mean I had never worked in publishing, but that didn't mean I could be an instant expert in the field within a week's time. I asked the CEO up front if that was a deal killer, and he assured me that it wasn't. This was an important, coveted position that hadn't turned over in more than a decade. He was eager to fill the spot, previously held by a communications executive who was well respected in New York media circles. He was looking for an aggressive communications person to help him relaunch the brand, so to speak, and build industry buzz. There was plenty of opportunity to promote the brand across the social media universe and get some excitement going with the mainstream press—my specialty.

The interview lasted an hour. In closing, the CEO said there were a few other people he was talking to, but that he'd like to set up a time for me to come back and speak in more detail.

While waiting for that to happen, I landed a phone interview with another high-profile company in the online financial world. They were seeking a senior-level director of communications to launch several new ventures, including a new mobile product. The person would lead all external communications for the company.

Problem solved. I was their man. I could have a job in less than three weeks, and although the company was based in Silicon Valley, this position could be worked from their New York offices. All was going according to plan. In both cases I was confident that I would be very successful in either of these roles, but that didn't mean I would ultimately be hired for the job . . .

And, oh, how prophetic that would prove to be. This expedition I was embarking on was to be a life-altering shift in my psyche that fed my soul with dread and depression that then led to feelings of hopelessness, shock, denial, and panic about my financial future; resentment toward my former employer; and, worst of all, anger toward myself. Over time, wrestling with those emotions proved time and again to be overwhelming, rendering me powerless to even get out of bed or take a shower.

I had set my expectations high for the call with this second company. I was prepared for the interview to go the way the first one had. As it turned out, it was 180 degrees from that. The director was a half hour late to the call. He said the job description no longer applied to the position. He was now looking for someone with a consumer and retail background. He asked me to describe a PR campaign I had spearheaded at my former employer. I answered the question; he asked for more details—and more. I kept explaining, and he wanted more. I ran out of details! It was absurd, but there was nothing I could do about it. You know when someone asks you a question or two and then feigns interest in your response but is really disinterested? That was what was going on. The interview was sinking like a boat anchor.

His next comment made me laugh. "The *right person* for this position will have more technical and engineering skills." It was strange to hear him say this: *the right person*. Didn't he know I had two prior calls with his HR department who vetted me for the position and thought I was—*the right person*? It was clear from my résumé alone that I wasn't an engineer. He kept telling me more about who he was looking for and how *the right person* will have this and have that—all details left off the job description.

Why was I sitting here talking to this guy with a bogus job description anyway? How could there be such a disconnect between him and HR? After fifteen minutes of this "interview," he said, "Dwain, I'm sorry, but I have to jump off. I'm dealing with a breaking news story on a press release we just sent out. It's been a pleasure talking with you. Do you have any questions?"

Do I have any questions? I thought he was joking. He had just conducted one of the worst interviews on planet Earth I had ever experienced in my life. Not only did I not get a chance to ask any questions, I didn't get three minutes to tell him what I thought I could do for him and the company.

"Well, I think if we could schedule another time to talk I could show you why I'm the right person you're looking for. You still don't know much about my background yet. Not from this call. Any chance of setting up another time to speak? I will make it worth your time," I said to him, knowing I may as well be talking to the wall.

"Let me talk to our HR people and get back to you. Have to run now." Click.

● **THE SECOND INTERVIEW** with the website company went better than the first. We talked about the role in more detail. I brought with me some talking points summarizing what I would do during my first ninety days on the job. During the interview, the CEO spoke as if I had the position already. He talked about managing the new PR agency he had recently hired. In closing, he asked whether I had time to meet with his HR director, always a great sign. I said I did.

I asked him, "What is your time frame on getting this position filled?"

"I'm looking to wrap this up in the next couple weeks if I can," he said. He then asked me about my timing. "Of course I don't know how much notice you might have to give, but I'm sure we can work around that," he said. These were all "buy" signals leading me to believe that we were closing in on an offer. He said he wanted me to come back one more time to meet the brains behind the website.

I spent nearly an hour with HR talking mostly about my international travels for AmeriCares, where I headed up communications in the early 1990s. It was a friendly conversation but light on technicalities, which concerned me. When I asked her what she thought the new communications leader needed to do to be successful at the company, she paused a few seconds and said, "My motto is: don't fix what ain't broke."

I thought, wow, *I need to introduce you to your CEO, because he's saying the exact opposite.*

Days melted into weeks before I finally sent the CEO an e-mail inquiring about our final meeting. I called him several times to no avail. He was dodging me. I started to get that sinking feeling— and for good reason. Several days after I left a third message for him, he shot me an e-mail. He apologized for not getting in touch, but he had decided to hire a woman with digital publishing experience. He went on to say that it was a tough decision and he valued my creativity, attitude, and even more my work ethic but that he felt he needed to go with a "template that will work in a by-the-book fashion."

Apart from it being a polite rejection letter, the note was a punch to my solar plexus. The HR lady gave it away though weeks before. They weren't prepared to bring in someone to shake things up or realize the CEO's true vision. Or did the CEO really have a vision in the first place? What I considered to be my Achilles' heel (not having come from the digital publishing world) hindered me as I thought it would, even though he said at the outset it wasn't a concern. He was playing it safe. Terms like *template* and *by-the-book fashion* were antithetical to what he had been saying to me for the past month. It was as if someone else stepped in at the last minute and made the final decision without taking into account the unique relationship he and I had developed over the months.

This was a rude awakening to the harsh reality of the brave new job market. I had my work cut out for me. I just missed out on a position for which I had a strong referral and was more than qualified. I was born to do that role, but it was not to be.

Not to fear. I had come close to landing a dream job, gotten practice interviewing at a high level, and had several more opportunities on the horizon. What I took away from the experience was how easy it was to get lulled into a false sense of security while interviewing. It's like a parallel universe. Just because *I* thought I was the best person for the job doesn't mean the company is going to *hire* the best person for the job. Go ahead, read that twice.

Peter Bell, New York City executive search veteran and founder of Peter Bell & Associates, says "best" is in the eye of the beholder and sadly mostly irrelevant. "It's one of the biggest myths out there that the best man or woman gets the job," Bell states matter-of-factly. "It's not the best person who gets the job, and it's not something you can measure as to why not. It's about a connection that is made. That's what it is."

So what happened to me? I had connected well with the CEO, and he was displaying all the signs that lead to an offer. "Of course, more than one person is going to be signing off on most hires, so that can work for or against you too. Don't think he was the only one necessarily calling the shots. Someone you never met in the organization could have knocked you out," Bell says.

I think it was the HR lady, but that's just me. Doesn't matter now. When in doubt blame it on HR. Regardless, I was on a roll, not to be discouraged from my grandiose ideas that I would be landing a job three weeks out of work. Pretty good for a guy who prided himself on going it alone—doing it his way without a formalized plan of attack or safety net, but rather forging forward through sheer willpower *and personal radiance*. I was also racing the clock because I wanted to show my former employer that I found a better, more respectable place to work. (My father dropped the bomb one day that they don't give a shit. The nerve.) This was not the humblest moment of my life.

Unfortunately, a huge helping of humble pie in the weeks and months ahead tested what I was made of like no other life experience before it. Unemployment in the Great Recession was the great equalizer. In a March 6, 2013, *New York Times* article, Catherine Rampell reported on how, despite a slowly improving economy, companies were still holding off hiring in significant numbers or were stringing along job applicants for weeks and months before making a decision—if they made one at all: "The hiring delays are part of the vicious cycle the economy has yet to escape: jobless and financially stretched Americans are reluctant to spend, which holds back demand, which in turn frays employers' confidence that sales will firm up and justify committing to a new hire."

Using what I call my job search rifle approach, I called a former colleague to see whether she could introduce me to some friends of hers at a company in New York I thought I was uniquely qualified for. She landed me a phone interview with a bitter corporate communications division head. I think part of the negativity was a result of her being turned down from a job at my former employer. Whatever the reason, she was insensitive to my plight. I let her take another ten minutes of my life I'll never get back to tell me why I wouldn't be hired at her company and then I thanked her for her time and hung up.

Nearly three months had passed, and I had been on half a dozen more interviews, sometimes making it to the second round. Job leads were becoming more difficult to locate, and the competition for the jobs out there was brutal. The economic reports said it all: more than twenty-three million people were now out of work or underemployed—many well-educated, middle-aged, white-collar workers. Adding to that, one of the world's largest search firms, Manpower, and the business-oriented social networking site LinkedIn published a survey that said eighty-two million employed people were also interested in new opportunities. One reason for this is more Americans are overworked because of staff reductions brought on by the recession.

Paroxysms of anger were replacing the sure-footed emotions I had at the outset of my search. I went from thinking, *I would be a great find* to *I'm not proud—I'll beg for a job if I have to.*

Friends who had traveled the unemployment road before me explained that coping with joblessness is similar to experiencing a death in the family and going through the five stages of grief. I was stuck in the anger stage. My emotions were running rampant, and I was becoming difficult to live with.

I asked pre-eminent career reinvention coach, author, and founder of the Reinvention Institute Pamela Mitchell whether what I was going through is to be expected. She says 50 percent of a job search revolves around writing cover letters, résumés, and going on interviews. The other 50 percent affects the head in ways we aren't prepared to deal with:

There is a huge emotional journey ahead of anyone when it comes to unemployment and the identity shifts you will experience. And the emotional side of unemployment is something that people tend not to talk about. People want to immediately talk tactics. No one spends time thinking about the emotional passage that has to happen. There is fallout that takes place, and people feel they are shifting to that anger-denial phase no matter how ready they are to deal with it emotionally.

I had been on the journey before, but not to this extent. In 2009, at the height of the recession, the boutique PR agency and small recruiting company I cofounded with a friend and my father in the late 1990s had been decimated, along with millions of other small businesses. We were not too big to fail.

In that case, I had a little time to wind down because I worked for myself. Even though we were not bringing in new clients, we still had projects in the works and were collecting the majority of our outstanding receivables. There was some cash coming in. While that was happening, I started looking for new job opportunities. I thought my best-case scenario would be to join a medium-sized company and head up its communications department. My business partners decided to make a go of the recruiting company on their own.

As I searched for work, it became apparent that I had never been unemployed because my résumé looked like a fifth grader had written it. It was disorganized and full of holes. Here I was, a professional communicator in the broadcast news and public relations business for most of my life, a man who made a living writing press releases and magazine articles, and my résumé was almost illegible. What was I going to do about it?

The Economy's Not All to Blame:
The Evolution of the Modern Corporation

How did we employees become so expendable in the first place? It's not just the economy, stupid—or is it? The overall constructs of the modern corporation didn't come into existence that long ago. Its evolution shines a light on the vulnerabilities that exist even today when it comes to job security, loyalty, and career longevity. Historically speaking, we've gone through three eras of the corporate way of life. We are in the midst of what some very smart career counselors say is the birth of a fourth epoch brought about by this crash. The corporation we know today didn't exist in the mid-1800s. Businesses back then were local entities, and the volume of economic activity took place in a relatively small geographic area. The dawn of the transcontinental railway changed all of that, allowing companies to set up offices in different parts of the country to take advantage of interstate commerce. In fact, the railroads became the first modern multiunit businesses. According to Alfred DuPont Chandler Jr., author of the Pulitzer Prize–winning book *The Visible Hand*, the railroads were the first to set up central and regional offices and layers of administrative infrastructure to manage workers. The modern manager was born.

By the 1920s corporations employed 80 percent of the American workforce and even inspired the thirtieth president of the United States, Calvin Coolidge, to quip during an address to the American Society of Newspaper Editors in Washington, DC, that the "the chief business of the American people is business."

After World War II came the age of the "the company man" as put forth in William H. Whyte Jr.'s influential book *The Organization Man*. Whyte documented how companies, starting in the 1950s, were able offer job security to a workforce that was willing to conform to the demands of the corporation—in essence be loyal to the firm at all cost, do what they tell you, and go where they tell you to go, no questions asked. For that the worker would have a job for life.

This dynamic worked for many years because of longer business cycles: companies needed to set in place strategies that lasted a decade or longer and thus needed employees to stick around and do the work. In those days people put in their thirty years and enjoyed routine raises, promotions, and myriad benefits. Around that same time, labor unions came into being to ensure hourly workers the same kind of job security. People rarely switched companies. It was almost unheard of to change industries. Staying loyal to the company as much as guaranteed employment and the ability to retire with a healthy pension.

Pension… what's that?

Veteran print and broadcast journalist and political commentator on *Morning Joe*, Mike Barnicle basks in the nostalgia surrounding the days of the fat pension. He recounts the time former Speaker of the House Thomas "Tip" O'Neill Jr. and his wife, Millie, visited President Gerald and First Lady Betty Ford at the White House on the second night Ford was in office. O'Neill told Barnicle that, during the course of dinner, Ford leaned over to him and said, "Do you have any idea what a bump in pay this job is for me and what it's going to mean for my pension?"

"I love this story on two levels," Barnicle tells me. "One, President Ford was a pretty good, regular guy, and the other element is that word—*pension*—is gone. You don't hear people talk about 'what's your pension today?' or 'how's your pension?' The word has disappeared."

The era of the organization man stayed much the same until the 1980s technology boom turned the corporate model on its head. This third period gave rise to the independent worker. The rules of business had changed, and Wall Street began rewarding companies for ditching long-term profitability for shorter-term gains. CEOs were forced to reduce expenses, and workers were ever increasingly being let go because employees were expensive. On top of that, Web 1.0 technology was streamlining operations, making it easier for companies to do more with fewer people, and overseas labor allowed them to pay much less to get more. Lifetime employment was out the window.

The world had suddenly become a very competitive place for workers. Along with the downside of the uncertainty and instability came an upside—for the first time workers were able to be more flexible about when and where they worked. Superstars were born who could pick the best projects and negotiate the best wages. People were becoming experts in their fields, so that if a position didn't work out at one company, they could work for another company down the street. That was job security 1980s-style.

By the late 1990s and early 2000s, the pace of change surged as technology increased exponentially, allowing industries to experience much shorter business cycles. Companies and industries that ascended in a fifteen-year window started to collapse.

By 2008 everything crashed. Real estate, banking, and other perceived safe industries saw the need to reinvent themselves to stay competitive, partly because technology had changed business models so drastically.

The Great Recession sees the United States entering a so-called fourth era of corporate and workforce reinvention, according to Pamela Mitchell. In her book *The 10 Laws of Career Reinvention*, she states, "In this era, lengthy job tenure has lost its value. It's not how long you last somewhere that counts; it's what you bring to the table. The people who will thrive in this new world order are those who can repeatedly and successfully transform themselves."

More on that in chapter 9.

2

WORK ETHIC

Unemployment Hurts
Because I Love to Work

As far back as I can remember, I loved to work. I was anything but lazy. I particularly loved manual labor. It gave me a sense of purpose. The accomplishment I felt after putting in a hard day of work electrified me. I think my work ethic was handed down to me from my grandfather Arthur. My father and I are both chips off the old block. My grandfather was one of the hardest-working men I knew, and I respected him for that, among many other qualities. A blue-collar man through and through, as many were from his generation, he was born on a farm in Illinois in 1910 where hard work was a way of life. He decided to leave the farm for a better life in California, but the Great Depression derailed those plans.

He and my grandmother raised three boys, and my grandfather settled in as a mill worker at a flour mill in downtown Los

Angeles. As a trained flour smutter, he stayed during World War II, as strict rationing of staple foods like bread, sugar, fats, and oils created a great demand for processed wheat to feed the troops and civilian population.

My grandfather spent his retirement enjoying the outdoors, hunting ducks in the central California basin and fishing on the Sacramento River. He was an avid sportsman, and I loved spending time with him. He taught me to hunt and fish and the meaning of hard work. He taught me about the importance of labor unions and how they protected guys like him from being exploited in the workplace.

He also understood the value of education, and he didn't want me to go into manual labor as he had done. He was so proud of me when I was accepted into the journalism school at USC.

From the time I was in junior high school, I worked odd jobs and always had full-time employment during the summer. By the time I was in high school, my best friend, Jeff Pennington, and I had learned to paint houses. His father was a fire chief, and he and other firemen painted to make extra money on their days off. They taught us the ropes our first summer in high school, and we went out and started our own interior and exterior painting business. To this day I don't know how or why our business took off as well as it did. I was confident that we did good, detailed work. We were meticulous, did a great job prepping before we painted, and cleaned up everything spic and span. Strictly by word of mouth, we had more jobs than we could handle. We weren't lowballing the market either. Like I said, I never understood our success. It was magical.

I loved the work and the freedom it provided. We were outdoors in the sunny Southern California climate and calling our own shots. After we finished painting an exterior, customers were often so happy they would find work for us to do indoors, like paint a bedroom or a hallway. Come fall we would go back to school with thousands of dollars in the bank. It was hard work, but I loved the independence. It also fueled an entrepreneurial flame that has guided me throughout my life.

As seniors in high school, Pennington and I did back-breaking work for a friend's father. We dug ditches, built decks, and landscaped properties he owned. Our friend's father also owned a commercial fishing boat in San Diego. The summer after graduating high school, he hired us to catch albacore tuna commercially. Unlike yellowfin tuna that school close to shore and are caught using purse seine nets, albacore are relatively solitary fish, living far out at sea, and can only be caught using rods and reels, lift poles and baited hooks that attach to a single longline that is then set at an appropriate depth. It's backbreaking work. Albacore are an elusive, fierce fighting fish. One minute you're into an acre of them, and the next minute they disappear. When the bite is on, it's not uncommon for every line in the water to have a hookup. Besides being one of the best-tasting fish in the ocean, albacore are fast swimmers, clocking in at sixty to seventy miles per hour. We would stay out seven to ten days at a time, fishing until we came back to shore and unloaded our smelly cargo overnight. Then back out we went. Again, the money was great, but this job did more to swear me off manual labor than any I had ever done before. There was never enough time to sleep, and I was prone to seasickness when the weather turned bad. My hands took a beating because the exposure to salt water kept them perpetually soft and susceptible to deep gashes from the filament fishing line we were constantly pulling on.

The following year I entered college, while my friend delayed going to school to work on another fishing boat in the Sea of Cortez in Baja California. The following summer he jumped ship again and was back in San Diego working on the *Pilikia*— Hawaiian for "trouble." I joined him for a month fishing albacore and harpooning swordfish for the boat owner's California specialty seafood chain of restaurants called the Fish Market.

After graduating from USC with a degree in broadcast journalism, I worked for several years as a producer and part-time reporter for a national satellite TV station in Texas. From there I moved to Connecticut, where I became an award-winning on-air television reporter. An adrenaline junkie at heart, I was always looking for the next big story when I wasn't covering features in some of the local southwestern Connecticut towns. I covered a few shootings and a train crash in my day, but most of the time I reported on school board meetings, local art exhibits, music festivals, and the death and destruction Mr. Happy Cat brought to one town's beachside endangered piping plover population.

Working late in the newsroom one evening, I received a phone call from a woman who was looking to tell the world about her struggle with a little-known disease called complex regional pain syndrome (CRPS), formerly known as reflex sympathetic dystrophy syndrome or causalgia, a chronic disease characterized by severe pain and suffering that worsens over time. With a little research I discovered that the disease was considered *the* most painful condition to live with, surpassing childbirth and amputations and scoring highest on the McGill pain scale (42 out of a possible 50). It was dreadful to contemplate, but the story was too great to pass up, and several of the worst cases lived in our viewing area.

I jumped on the story right away and learned that Yale–New Haven Hospital in Connecticut and Thomas Jefferson University Hospitals in Center City Philadelphia were breaking new ground in CRPS research and pain management. I begged my news director to give me and a cameraman a week to work on the story. It was asking a lot, because he could neither spare the budget or manpower, but he signed off on it anyway, and I began lining up patients to speak with in Connecticut and at the hospital in Philadelphia. To this day I think it was one of the best stories I ever worked on. It was also one of the most difficult because of the scale of human suffering this disease wrought on these innocent people. I worked hard to tell their story as accurately and compassionately as possible to as many people as possible and to draw awareness to this horrible malady in the hope more researchers would take notice and work to find a cure. In one case I documented a patient whose pain in her arm was so severe surgeons decided to amputate to relieve the suffering. Weeks later the patient developed phantom limb pain. Doctors ended up surgically implanting an intrathecal pump that administered small quantities of morphine to ease the suffering.

However, the story that changed my life forever was when I begged my way onto a cargo jet flying medical supplies and emergency doctors to the capital city of Yerevan in Armenia on behalf of AmeriCares. The organization was responding with lifesaving supplies to an earthquake in the northern region of Spitak, Armenia (then part of the Soviet Union), that had taken at least twenty-five thousand lives. The region's poorly constructed Soviet buildings sustained heavy damage or collapsed completely. The Soviets were not prepared for a disaster of this scale. Most of the hospitals in the area were destroyed, and the freezing winter temperatures rendered the Soviet relief effort useless. So Mikhail Gorbachev formally asked the United States for humanitarian help, the first time a Soviet leader had done so since World War II. AmeriCares became the first private relief agency to respond, and as it turned out I became the only TV reporter in the Western world to have boots on the ground for this history-making relief effort.

The human suffering was palpable. The earthquake, 6.8 on the Richter scale, destroyed 100 percent of the homes and left more than half a million people in Spitak alone homeless in one day's time. As sad as the story was, as a journalist I'd learned to compartmentalize my personal life and set aside biases and emotions to cover the story as accurately as possible. For a regional Connecticut-based TV reporter, this was definitely the big leagues. I was in and out of the country with my story before the big boy US news networks even arrived.

Back home we ran the story as a three-part series. The program resonated with AmeriCares's founder Bob Macauley in a way other news stories of the catastrophe hadn't. It drew tons of attention to his organization in and around southwestern Connecticut, some of the most affluent neighborhoods in the country. He noticed an uptick in donations from the region as the organization continued to support disaster victims weeks after the initial airlift of supplies. AmeriCares returned to Armenia two more times, even airlifting an injured child who needed special surgery that could best be accomplished in the United States.

A week after the story aired, I received a surprise phone call from Bob's PR man asking me to come to his offices for a meeting. We met for a half hour, and he praised me for the coverage his organization had received and the windfall it generated. Then, out of nowhere, he asked me to consider joining the organization to help head up his public relations efforts. Not the bashful type, he asked me what I was earning as a TV reporter and said whatever it was he would double it. *No kidding*, I thought. I could hardly afford rent, and here was this multimillionaire philanthropist offering me an instant solution to all life's problems—at that time, anyway.

But this meant ditching the journalism career that I had studied for and was making a go at it. I was working hard to land a job in a top ten news market. I spent years dreaming of being the next Tom Brokaw or working as a foreign correspondent for CBS news, the home that William S. Paley built, where broadcasting pioneers Edward R. Murrow and Eric Sevareid made history reporting during the Blitz on London during World War II. *The Camera Never Blinks*, by CBS's Dan Rather, was the impetus for my getting into journalism in the first place. He was the best. Nobody better than Rather in his prime.

I had already made up my mind on the spot. I would take the job at AmeriCares. I couldn't help thinking this would be the experience of a lifetime.

That turned out to be an understatement. Working at AmeriCares was like no job I'd ever had before or will have again. Timing was everything. I was single and didn't mind living out of a backpack in some of the most godforsaken places on earth. My job was to tell our story to the world to raise the funds necessary to deliver lifesaving medicines and supplies to those most in need after a natural disaster or during a manmade one like war. In those days before the Internet and e-mail, most of my time was spent calling and faxing journalists, producers, and TV reporters in hopes of getting our staff in the paper or on the morning network news shows. Most of the time I could provide TV stations with video I shot covering our airlift into disaster areas.

They loved the free footage. What they grew to love even more was when we offered seats on the plane. We could fly journalists right to the hot spots they so clamored to cover, and we could piggyback on their reporting on how they got there and the good work one private US humanitarian group was doing. It was gratifying to me from a professional standpoint because as a PR person I was utilizing a lot of the same skills I used as a journalist. I used my writing skills to produce press releases, newsletters, and video scripts for documentaries we produced. I also organized press conferences and was the agency's chief spokesperson. I saw the world like nobody's business, helping to save thousands of lives and working with world leaders, some of the greatest volunteer doctors in the country, and some of America's most respected media personalities like Peter Jennings and Dr. Bob Arnot.

————

I know gratitude is the best medicine to fight away the blues. It especially helps me keep perspective on what I'm going through with my job search. I achieve that kind of grounding when every so often I take a few moments and reflect upon my days working at AmeriCares. They were some of the most fun days of my life and some of the most heartbreaking and life threatening. I can't help but think sometimes that no matter what I go through during this time of unemployment, no matter how tough it gets or down in the dumps I get, I lived a life at AmeriCares few people on earth will ever have the opportunity to experience.

I was part of a group of humanitarians who helped millions of people survive the aftermath of devastating natural disasters and the atrocity of war, riots, and, the granddaddy of them all, genocide. When I'm most blue I find a modicum of comfort thinking about how I was part of something special that helped ease the pain of my fellow man—whether for a day or a lifetime. I made a small difference in the world, and I'll make it through this time of need too.

I think what AmeriCares's founder, Bob Macauley, brilliantly accomplished more than anything else was to *merchandise* hope to the world, wrapped in the American flag.

We brought eternal optimism to the world—pick a spot, any spot on the map that was suffering—in the form of medicine, food, and volunteer doctors to help ameliorate pain and misery. We showed people of all faiths, nationalities, and persuasions that somebody out there in this big old world cares about their well-being, no matter how badly the odds were stacked against them.

And so, when I arrived on the tarmac of Kigali's Gregoire Kayibanda International Airport in the middle of the worst geno-cide in modern history, little did I know how badly the odds were stacked against *my* making it home alive. It was 1994 and Rwanda had blown its stack. Best known to Americans as the land of the majestic mountain gorillas, Rwanda had become the land of ma-niac machete-wielding Hutus intent on killing every living Tutsi in this tiniest of African nations. The bloodshed began after Rwandan president Juvénal Habyarimana and Burundian president Cyprien Ntaryamira were shot down as their plane approached the airport in the capital of Kigali. To this day nobody knows for sure who brought the plane down, but regardless of the cause the act set off an immediate retaliation against the Tutsi population living in the country (the second-largest population in Rwanda next to the Hutus). Anti-Tutsi militias set up roadblocks across Rwanda and slaughtered every Tutsi they could find until they were driven away by rebel Rwandan Patriotic Front troops.

When the dust settled more than 80 percent of the country's Tutsi population—nearly a million people—were exterminated in the most efficient and complete genocide of modern times, all in less than a hundred days. To give you some perspective, if you lined up the dead end to end, they would stretch across three-quarters of the United States.

Rwanda had become a massive killing field to say the least.

I was in the country to document our relief efforts near the border of Goma, Zaire (now the Democratic Republic of the Congo), where we set up several makeshift hospital structures in the hills of Rwanda and intercepted tens of thousands of injured and dying refugees returning home from refugee camps in neighboring Zaire. One of the structures was used as a quarantine ward, one for women and children, and another for men. It was a crude setup by Western standards.

I had brought newspaper and magazine journalists, network news videographers and photographers to record the work we were doing. Volunteer doctors from the Mayo Clinic, Yale, and the Stamford Hospital in Connecticut were working around the clock saving lives, treating mostly jagged and infected machete wounds. Many of the children were malnourished and dehydrated. One little boy in the camp had become our mascot. We called him Ozzi. We never knew his real name because his parents, like many Tutsis during the genocide, took refuge in their church, thinking it sacred ground and a safe refuge. Hutus lit the churches on fire and hacked to death the unarmed Tutsis who tried to escape a certain smoky death.

Ozzi just showed up one day wearing a red T-shirt and nothing else. He couldn't have been more than six years old. He was the healthiest kid in the camp, and he stayed with us in a cinder-block guesthouse we had taken over on the property. We wanted to take him home with us when we returned to the States, but at that time it was against the law to adopt children from Rwanda. I think about that little boy every once in a while with sadness and hope in my heart and wonder what happened to him and whether he's alive today. I will never know.

After several days of reporting at our hilltop hospital site, the journalists and I loaded up a van with camera gear and human cargo and set off for the border-town-turned-makeshift-refugee-staging-area in Goma where we were also providing for a small children's clinic.

Off in the distance I could see we were coming up on a check-point. This was the border crossing into Zaire. I warned our group to leave their cameras down. Taking pictures at the crossing would incite a riot among the young soldiers guarding the roadblock. We rolled to a stop next to a small concrete guard post on the side of the road that housed three young men in uniform armed with AK-47s. Another ten young soldiers stood in front of and off to the side of our vehicle. They were all chewing khat, a drug derived from the leaves of a wild East African shrub. To my disbelief my photographers were snapping away as quickly as they could. The video camera was recording everything.

They were doing what came instinctively to them, but they were also digging our grave without knowing it. I had spent years traveling in war zones like Bosnia, Eritrea, and Somalia, where you had to be vigilant about the customs of the country you were visiting and use common sense to stay alive. In this case it wasn't enough for me to simply tell my new cameramen friends to keep their cameras put away until we crossed the border—that in some countries in Africa you can be hanged (or worse) for taking pictures of military installations like border crossings. I also realized I wasn't traveling with hardened foreign correspondents on this trip. I was working with *People* magazine, a couple of New York newspaper cameramen, and a local New York TV news crew.

We were pulled from the van and stripped of our cameras and bags. One soldier seemed to take charge, screaming at us in French, and then others joined in poking us in the ribs and shoulders with their rifles. They were spitting as they yelled, corralling us into a tighter ball. A couple of us fell to our knees. I stayed standing. They were trying to push us to the ground. That was the weakest position you could be in. I learned long ago, once an aggressor gets you on your knees or stomach, it takes very little for them to finish you off execution-style. They have nothing to lose, and these soldiers had nothing to lose this day. How hard would it be for them to shoot us in the back of the head and leave us for dead on the side of the road to rot in the sun? They had become accustomed to death.

Our problem, among many at the moment, was we couldn't communicate with the soldiers. I didn't speak French, and to the best of my knowledge no one in my group was fluent. But out of the blue our freelance magazine reporter named Isabelle, who was filing stories for *People*, yelled in French at one of the young soldiers pointing a rifle at my head to lower his weapon. She identified someone in the group who would engage with her, surprising since women are shown little or no respect by authority figures in war zones. I was stunned by how aggressive she had become, admonishing two and three of the young soldiers at a time. Her survival reflexes were on full parade.

Of course, we had nothing to lose and she was our only hope of getting out of this mess alive—or was she?

If you've been in the international humanitarian relief business long enough and had enough confrontations with gun-toting, drugged-out warlords, you learned early on the benefits of traveling with a backpack of Marlboro cigarettes. They are the currency of choice in most third- and fourth-world countries and can usually turn the most belligerent foe into a friend. Same goes for Hershey's chocolate bars, but cigarettes travel much better in the African heat. I've used Hershey's Kisses to much success in countries like Russia and the former Yugoslavia.

I had packed cartons of cigarettes for our journey to Goma, but the soldiers had confiscated my bag of contraband along with the camera gear. I pointed out to Isabelle where the bag was on the side of the road and asked her if she could convince one of the soldiers to allow me to retrieve the bag. She explained to one of the soldiers the precious cargo in my gray backpack, and sure enough he walked over and opened it to confirm the story.

It was almost magical what happened next. One by one the soldiers started to smile. Their boyish mannerisms started to come through as they lowered their rifles and relaxed their shoulders as they waited for me to start handing out packs of cigarettes. It was as if Santa had come to town. By instinct I could feel the collective relief of our group as the soldiers peeled off the cellophane to get to the cigarettes. As they started lighting up, mixing the buzz of tobacco with the khat they had been chewing all day, it struck me how surreal and how dramatically the mood had changed at the border crossing. All I could think about was how critical it was for us to leave while the going was good.

And then the unthinkable happened. One of the boy soldiers insisted, at gunpoint no less, that we all take a group photo before they let us go. Was this a joke? Were they now going to shoot us?

With cigarettes hanging out of their mouths we lined up along the border as one of my photographers snapped off a dozen shots. We all shook hands, collected our gear, and loaded up the van. One of the soldiers lifted the gate to let us pass.

Now, surviving this job search is proving to be a different story!

3

WHO AM I?

The Inner Game of Dealing with
Insecurity and Uncertainty

It's week four of the job search. I came across a posting on the Internet that piqued my interest. The local cable company was looking for door-to-door sales reps to call on homeowners who were using a competitor's service in an effort to convert them. I always fancied myself as good at sales. My father was a successful salesman, and the skills he acquired in that field allowed him to become an even more successful business owner. I picked up many of his skills by listening to him talk about his experiences working for Xerox back in the late 1960s and 1970s, when Xerox was the Microsoft or Apple of its day. It was a stressful place to work, but everyone wanted to work there, so the salespeople were forever being pushed to close more deals and open more business channels. My dad was the personification of a "hunter-gatherer," scooping up new customers and closing deals in downtown Los

Angeles, where he held the number one sales position for several years, calling on clients in LA's tallest building at the time, the United California Bank Building. Fascinated by the training he went through to become more effective, I learned at a young age that sales was a strategic, numbers-driven endeavor. The numbers part didn't appeal to me, but the communications aspect of the job interested me greatly. It was all about the art of persuasion, gamesmanship, and taking little steps to get customers to come to *their* own conclusion that it was in *their* best interest to say, "Yes, we'll buy it!" Over the dinner table, Dad would tell my brother and me about the strategic closes he used to encourage buy signals. There was the companion close, the concession close, the puppy dog close, and—one of my favorites—the Ben Franklin close. Known for his common sense, Franklin developed this logical method of helping the prospective customer make a yes-or-no decision, and Franklin used the method himself to make decisions. In practice my father would have the prospect draw a line down the center of a piece of paper. On the left side the customer would write down all the reasons for the decision. On the right side of the paper the prospect would write down all of the arguments against the decision. When completed, the customer simply counted the number of arguments for and then compared that to the arguments against; most of the time the reasons for taking a certain action became overwhelmingly clear. In the hands of a skilled salesman like my father, yes's outnumbered no's two to one.

I knew instinctively that the Franklin technique would work best for flipping cable service customers to a new provider. I e-mailed the human resources department of the company a cover letter and hastily written résumé that focused on my sales and business development skills. I drew on my experience running my

PR and talent recruiting business. To my surprise I received a return e-mail inviting me to interview for the job. I was giddy with excitement. This could potentially take me completely off the career track I'd been on for years, and the thought of a fresh start was intoxicating. I had no idea what the job paid but relished the thought of trying something new. I assumed there was potential to make a lot of money because it probably paid mostly commission, which favored people who worked hard and smart. The downside is you only eat what you kill (close deals), and if you don't kill consistently, you don't eat much. I put that out of my mind. The company offered great benefits from day one. That was critical to me and my family, who were making do with COBRA insurance that cost a fortune.

Whew—what a sense of relief! Landing this interview gave me breathing room to set up other interviews in my chosen field. It was a fallback that, if all else failed, would be a stepping-stone to something better.

The interview lasted three hours. The company called in five candidates that day, and in the end I was offered the job. I couldn't wait to call my wife and tell her the good news. I was proud. I had landed a new job in this horrible economy with a company that was excited to have me. They valued my experience and skills.

My wife saw it differently. In her supportive, let-me-down-gently sort of way, she counted off the reasons why this job wasn't a good fit. "Think about the constant rejection you will experience going door-to-door in the scorching summer heat and freezing winter asking people to buy something they don't want or need," she calmly said. Visions of trudging through snow knocking on the doors of rich people who aren't home all day started to sink in. And I hate humidity. How would I feel walking the streets in ninety-five degree heat with 80 percent humidity wearing a collared shirt and lugging armfuls of brochures? Was this the best use of my West Coast Ivy League education?

I had simply focused on landing a new job, like the hunter-gatherer father who went before me bagging the wooly mammoth in the form of a paycheck. What was I thinking?

I brought my situation to a career coach for his expert advice. I'm glad I did. Not that I didn't believe Colleen, but who listens to his wife? Paul Stuhlman is a twenty-five-year job search and outplacement veteran who has helped executives like me land new jobs as quickly and painlessly as possible. He appreciated my enthusiasm for bagging a new job. He happens to be the most encouraging and hopeful person I've ever known. When I first met him, he even professed to be in the "hope business." Good thing, because he also said this: "I've never seen the job market this bad in my entire career. There have been blips and periods of time when the job market dipped, such as 9/11 and things like that. The tech boom and bust was a bad time too, but this is the worst."

After reviewing my career history, he tells me,

You're taking that cable job over my dead body. Now if you're saying to me, "I hate communications—I now hate corporate life, I hate public relations, I want to do something different like door-to-door selling and have been thinking about doing this for a while, what do you think about cable TV?"—I would say, yeah, what the hell, give it a go.

But I think what you are telling me is you're desperate for a job, and what you're really wanting is another meaningful job that provides a handsome compensation package that would come with another vice president of communications title, but oh, by the way, the cable company asked me if I wanted to go sell services door-to-door.

Okay . . . he's got a point. If people got rich selling cable TV, there'd be a lot of people knocking on doors selling cable TV. Stuhlman helped me realize the overriding issue: my fear of unemployment was clouding my judgment. As far as he was concerned, I may as well have told him I was taking a job as the second-shift manager at McDonald's on Main Street. Stuhlman offered another approach: "Give the search a try for a while." He gave me a D+ for conducting a comprehensive, well-disciplined, organized job search. That was generous. I gave myself an F. Besides, how could he grade me on something I hadn't really initiated or even had the first inkling how to do? I would soon learn that looking for a job, and learning to do it the correct way, is not only a job in itself but is also the most psychologically challenging and draining experience I was ever forced to confront. I think it would be fair to say that nearly 95 percent of us who are reading this, highly paid executives included, haven't a clue how to conduct a successful search. That's not a put-down. It's just a fact. And why *would* you know how to conduct a strategically robust job search? Many of us have worked our entire life uninterrupted, seamlessly changing jobs to suit our interests and financial requirements. I was a mole in a hole until Stuhlman showed me the light of day. This book is worth its weight in gold if you follow the suggestions on how to "work" at landing a new job or transitioning to a new lifestyle that might not include a job at all. The only disclaimer is there's no guarantee as to when that might happen! I guarantee the journey will make you

a stronger, more resilient, more aware person, someone apprecia-
tive of what you have and attuned to how you can help others
who are drowning in the unemployment pool.

———

Maybe one day I'll look back and say, "I wish I'd never met
Paul Stuhlman because I would've made a lot of money
selling cable, launched a new career, and lived happily ever after."
The truth is he saved me from myself. His mission in life is to
convince people like me to do what is most difficult in this economy—and that is to embrace the uncertainty of the job search,
no matter how scary that situation is, and to start thinking more
strategically about developing an intelligent action plan.

I left Stuhlman's office and stopped at Panera Bread to grab a
coffee to go. Restaurants like these have become rent-free offices
for thousands of unemployed folks who can tap into free Wi-Fi
and suck down discounted coffee refills—one person's bust is another person's boom!

I was in a hurry. The line was long. I was one person away
from placing my order when the guy in front of me went into
a trance-like stupor studying the menu board. He was trying to
decide between the Cuban chicken panini or the asiago roast beef
sandwich with smoked cheddar, lettuce, tomatoes, red onions, and
creamy horseradish sauce on an asiago cheese demi. He was killing
me. "Boy, lunch is always the biggest decision of my day," he said
to nobody in particular.

Really? Seriously? I'm out of work, going broke by the second,
waiting for a stupid paper cup to pour some coffee in, used to
making big decisions, managing teams of people and multimil-
lion-dollar budgets, running small companies, rubbing elbows

with world leaders and celebrities like Elton John, Michael Jackson, and George H. W. Bush, and this guy was making a career out of whether to order a hot or cold sandwich.

This was turning into a scene right out of *Curb Your Enthusiasm*. How cool would it be to go to the source, the creator of *Curb* and *Seinfeld*, and get Larry David's take on how he dealt with unemployment during his early show business career? David is a good friend of Mika's, and when she told him I was writing this book he suggested I give him a buzz for a different perspective on being unemployed. Maybe my Panera experience would be fodder for a new show. David told me his advice for people like me is to do what he did: become an expert at *doing nothing*. Sounds like an episode out of Seinfeld to me.

"You have to get through your day and feel like you've accomplished something and yet you've accomplished nothing, knowing you've accomplished nothing!" David said in his signature overanalytical, Brooklyn-accented, neurotic tone.

So, getting through the day—what's the best way to do this? First, you can't get up early. That exacerbates the problem. You need to go to bed late and sleep late.

Why is that important?

I went to sleep at 4:00 in the morning. I got up at 12:00 p.m., so by the time I finished breakfast and read the newspaper it was already going on 1:30 or 2:00 o'clock, so now—if it's winter and what's left of daylight—most of the day's already gone. And if you get through days without feeling too much like a loser then you're way ahead of the game.

What you need to do is make it to 4 o'clock. The hours between 2:30 and 4:00 o'clock are the tough hours for the unemployed. You have to somehow make it through that—make a few phone calls, do a crossword puzzle—now it's 4:20 and people are starting to leave work—so now you're done. Now you're just a guy who has finished his day as if you were working.

"What do you do when you finish working?" I ask him.

You go home, have dinner and you get through the night. You're not bringing in any cash, so you're collecting unemployment hopefully, and you're alienating friends by borrowing money, and at this point your parents are a mess. If it weren't for the money factor it wouldn't be so bad.

So, in a nutshell, my advice . . . sleep late!

The Oh Boy Moment—This Is Harder Than I Thought

The "oh boy" moment of how adversely unemployment was affecting me came in late June when the kids were home for the summer. My severance had dried up, and my younger daughter wanted to go to sleepaway camp for the first time in her life at a cost of $2,500. She is an angel who never asks for anything, and going away to camp was a dream that we had promised to deliver on—before I got canned. It was a lot of money to spend, considering I was now jobless. I was anxious about being home with the kids. I was compounding my negative feelings because I kept telling myself I should be enjoying this "quality" time with the kids and family. It's summertime. I should be taking them swimming, on bike rides, hikes, and family trips. The reality is, lurking in the frontal lobe area of my brain was this nagging voice that said, *Hey loser, you should be working, not chasing butterflies with the kids.* I felt guilty running errands during the day, like I shouldn't be seen out and about. I shouldn't be at Trader Joe's in the afternoon or at Stop and Shop or picking up the dry cleaning. I should be at work! That's where I HAVE to be. Instead I'm out doing all of the things that need to be done to make the family run when my wife is working two part-time jobs. I can't just become a hermit.

The summer was tearing me apart. Emotionally, I wasn't great. I wasn't experiencing complete and abject mental collapse, but, with friends and in social settings, unemployment seemed to dominate the conversation, further triggering my mood swings. Unemployment had become a second skin I could no longer shed.

By midsummer I started doing more work to prepare myself for interviews, spending even more time sitting in front of the computer thinking, *All right, now it's time to find a job. For real. What's the first thing I'm going to do? I'm going to start thinking about starting now! Just start. Oh wait, I have to move the sprinkler.*

It turned out that there were two things I needed to do immediately: get my résumé buffed out (I had so many versions of it by now I was getting confused) and polish up my LinkedIn profile. For a lot of freshly minted middle-aged career seekers, LinkedIn was still a mystery social networking place where people were going to make sure everything added up on their work history (do the dates match up or is the person just bullshitting?). Even the term *social network* sends a chill down the spine of millions of middle-aged job seekers. With the help of LinkedIn, it was time I rekindled long-lost business relationships to help me find a job.

In her critically acclaimed book *The Power of Real-Time Social Media Marketing*, social media guru Beverly Macy along with coauthor Teri Thompson detailed the evolution of the way brands and individuals have come to leverage social media to strengthen their message, listen to customers, and effectively measure results. Macy tells me many fortysomethings are behind the times when it comes to embracing social media, but they're not alone. She spends a good part of her time traveling around the country teaching Fortune 100 companies ways to be more social. I joked with Macy when we met for lunch in New York that my thirteen-year-old daughter could teach Social Networking 101. She said that's no joke. We need to start thinking like teenagers if we're going to stay relevant in this anemic economy.

"LinkedIn, Pinterest, Facebook: these are all very powerful social media platforms. What I try to help people understand is they are simply tools like any other tool that help us communicate, connect, and transact," Macy explains to me. "I think a lot of job seekers, excluding recent college graduates, who are desperately feeling the ill effects of this job market don't realize that corporations use social media to find talent every day. HR professionals are using tools like LinkedIn to find new employees. They attend conferences learning how to better use these tools to find people like you, so you'd better learn how to get on their radar screen."

Macy says there is a marked divide between people who have taken the time to learn how to use social media and people who have dug in their heels and said social media is stupid, a passing fad, or who justified their objection by claiming there aren't enough built-in privacy features to make it safe. Whatever mythology you adhere to, she emphasizes that the social networking ship has left the dock: if you aren't on board, you will be left behind in ways that could set you back months if not years in executing a successful search. In this market, that's the kiss of death. Believe me, you are not alone if you feel confused by the prospect of educating yourself on what social media is and how to use it. I am here to say it is not the black art many may think it might be. It is, however, something that is always changing and evolving. Think of social media as nothing more than a contemporary way of communicating. That's all it really is. Social media simply helps people and businesses talk to each other and share information.

Macy's goal is to make sure fiftysomethings aren't left behind. I attended a presentation she gave at the St. Regis in Manhattan in October 2012 for City National Bank, a large California bank with a sizable presence in New York City that caters to the arts and entertainment world—mainly Broadway and the theater industry. The bank had invited its most important customers—wealth managers, attorneys, and client agents—to learn more about how small and large companies are leveraging social media to improve the bottom line. I could tell by the questions asked after the presentation that the whole concept of social media—the concept of someone tweeting five times a day about who their favorite singer was or where they had their nails done—was still a foreign if not banal concept, but Macy took it in stride. She kept hammering home the message that people need to realize these platforms are about giving a company or a customer a competitive edge with their ability to share, search, transact, interact, and push things around in new ways—and that this kind of human interaction is never going away. Companies are opening up new channels and making boatloads of money by harnessing the power of social media marketing. One example: the American Red Cross was able to use social channels and text-messaging technology to raise $33 million in real-time donations for the earthquake victims in Haiti. Today a customer can tweet a complaint to a company in real time, and that company can fix the problem on the spot, if it so chooses, more than likely keeping that person as a customer for life. What's more amazing, marketers can take advantage of all these innovative ways to meet and exceed market demands using Facebook, Twitter, YouTube, and other sites—all for free!

I asked Macy how many people she thought understood the real power of social media.

I would go as far as to say that less than 20 percent of middle-aged people who now find themselves out of work due to this difficult economy have an understanding of what social media is or how to use it to help them find their next job. It's terrible.

Some people in their late forties are starting to get a clue about social media because they are not finding work and they are going to seminars and they're going to networking events and hearing from others that they need to get on LinkedIn, but the frustrating thing is a lot of people will say, "I've done all that and my phone still isn't ringing."

More on that in a minute.

In addition to her speaking engagements, Macy teaches an extension course in social media marketing at UCLA. "I usually have a hundred people in the class. Many will come down to me, and they will sort of confidentially say, 'I'm scared. On the one hand I took your class because I'm really worried, and on the other I'm excited because I'm learning about all this, but I feel like everybody's talking a new language.'"

"What do you tell them?" I ask.

"I say, 'That's because they *are* speaking a new language. So congratulations to you for being here. This is your first step on the road to RELEVANCY!'"

The Résumé Is Dead… Sort Of

So much for a new language; I am also learning to pretty much kiss the résumé goodbye. It has been replaced by the LinkedIn profile. The LinkedIn profile looks like a résumé but it's not the CV of the past. Macy likens it to an "enhanced" résumé, because it's searchable, customizable, and shareable. Those three things make it dynamic and easily accessible to anyone. Employers who are looking for workers no longer have to ask for résumés up front. They can passively search out and find (or destroy) your profile on LinkedIn. Once a company is interested in your skill set, they can reach out and ask you to send over a résumé.

The next important thing is to make sure your résumé doesn't read like an obituary; that it doesn't simply list in chronological order one boring job assignment after another. You want it to position you in a way that focuses on your experience and opens you up to more opportunities. I was learning to present myself as "job-specific ready"; otherwise, the employer will just pigeonhole me into the same-old, same-old job I've been doing for seven or eight years.

"There are a lot of people who don't understand this new landscape," Macy says. "They go out to LinkedIn and recreate their old résumé, and they say, 'How come nobody's calling me?' I tell them that there are a bunch of reasons why nobody's calling—of course, one of the most brutal reasons is a lot of companies are still not hiring yet—but we can't control that."

So what can we control?

The first thing she recommends is to ditch the objectives section on your résumé or your LinkedIn profile. In the old days, like way, way, way back in the mid-1990s, many résumés still started with an "Objectives" subhead at the top, right under your name, address, and phone number. Today nobody cares about your objectives. (I'm starting to think nobody cares about me, period, but that's another book.) What people—read: employers—do care about is what value you bring that first day on the job.

"It has totally flipped," remarks Phil Cannon, who recently retired after a forty-three-year career as an award-winning sales executive for Xerox. Cannon specialized in complex sales of Xerox's flagship products to the LA County government, corporations, and professional service firms. He can attest to what it takes for new recruits to get a foothold in a place like Xerox. "There used to be so much employment out there that you needed to tell a potential employer why you want the job—how and where you want to grow—but it is meaningless today. All the employer wants now is a value proposition. I tell people replace your objectives with a value proposition. How are you going to hit the ground running on day one and contribute to the bottom line?"

So what is this value proposition? Macy says to think of social media as the ultimate personal branding tool. LinkedIn is the perfect place to state your elevator pitch, and it needs to be stated very clearly, like two paragraphs. I have to start tooting my own horn, she told me. In the past it was always left to the employer to single somebody out and say, "Joe has done such a great job we're going to give him a plaque."

That has been reversed. Now it's up to you to say, "I've done a great job and I've contributed to the company in these ways . . . "

"This is very uncomfortable for a lot of people. It is a complete shift in mind-set," Cannon notes. "This is where the salesperson that lurks inside us all—no matter what career you're in—needs to take center stage and put a stake in the ground."

Macy nails it for what it is: "bragging is now branding!"

I ask Stephanie Nelson, a social media marketing expert based in Charlotte, North Carolina, what her experience is in helping older job seekers get with the program:

> Personal branding is more of a foreign concept to middle-aged workers in the workforce who are deciding either on their own to change careers or somebody else has decided to change it for them. People need to think about how they appear online. If you Google your name, what shows up? And are you okay with what shows up?
>
> You want to show your personality, but you also want to show your expertise. If you're a social media person, you want to show that you're active on Google+, Twitter, Facebook, and Pinterest; pretty much wherever you want to be seen as an expert.
>
> For example, if you're a CPA, you want to make sure your LinkedIn profile shows that you're active on CPA-type groups on the site, and you want to make sure that all of your work history is there that proves your worth as a CPA. But you have to understand, you're not just a CPA, and you want to include

some hobbies, like you're a CPA who enjoys fly fishing; you need to fill out that brand so that people can see there are many facets to your personal brand.

Still not convinced? Here are a few more reasons online branding is so important:

- 70 percent of hiring managers surveyed say they've rejected a candidate based on information they've found online. —*Washington Post*, 1/28/10
- 37 percent of employers use Facebook to prescreen applicants.—*Huffington Post*, 4/12/12
- 91 percent of recruiters use social networks to evaluate job applicants.—2011 Reppler Survey
- Employers admit they're looking for résumé exaggerations and whether an applicant would be a good fit for their culture.

Nelson says there are other ways to optimize your digital footprint. One way to improve your online image is to "push the bad stuff down" by signing up for all of the major social channels (Twitter, Google+, Facebook, Pinterest, LinkedIn) that common search engines like Google, Yahoo, and Bing can find. This content, which you control, will then start to show up higher on search pages.

Another thing Nelson advises: "Be conscious of who your audience is and who you are hoping will find you. If you're trying to find a job, then recruiters and people in that vein will be looking towards LinkedIn. LinkedIn is considered a search engine now."

Speaking of search engines, today's traditional résumé needs to speak a different language than it did, say, fifteen years ago when you actually used it last. As mentioned earlier, an objectives statement is a thing of the past. "Seeking an opportunity to expand my knowledge and experience and to assist in the continued improvement of the organization. An aspiring team player, hard-working and dedicated professional who wants to meet the challenges posed in the industry and to contribute towards the growth of the organization along with self-motivation." Can you believe we used to put stuff like that in a résumé? Read it again. It says absolutely nothing. "I've got news for you: it's not going to get read," Macy says.

More to the point, that old-style résumé isn't optimized with keywords for search engines to find it once you send it to a company for review.

Search engines for résumés? Optimized? Let me explain.

Most of us by now have heard of the term SEO as it applies to Web 2.0. SEO is short for *search engine optimization*, which is a technique used to increase the amount of visitors to a website with a high ranking on the results page of a search engine like Google, Bing, Yahoo, and the rest. SEO helps improve the chances that the site will be found by the search engine and, thus, found by you and me.

Today job seekers need to optimize their résumés to make it through the employer's applicant tracking systems (ATS). This SEO-type system helps recruiters search your résumé using keywords to simplify the selection process and identify top candidates for interviews. Hypothetically, you could be the perfect candidate, with all of the right experience, but never be considered for the job because of poor choices in or lack of keywords.

The best way to come up with the right keywords is to scan the company's website and the description of the job you're applying for. What employers use in a job posting is almost always what they will use in a keyword search. Put yourself in the employers' shoes and write down what you think they will be searching for when hunting through their databases for candidates—skills, experience, education, certificates, etc. . . . all perfect keywords. For example, if the description says "MBA preferred," the system will search to see if your résumé lists an MBA. Recruiters tell me to avoid soft skill keywords like teamwork, attitude, enthusiasm; these are rarely picked up by the software.

"Don't pack your résumé with too many keywords, and don't add keywords that your background can't support," says executive search expert Peter Bell. "You need to submit the most accurate portrayal of yourself possible that specifically pertains to the exact job requirements listed in the job description." Bell says don't worry if your résumé is longer than one page. In his experience, for higher-level job positions you can typically use as many pages for your résumé as needed. He cautions to be smart about it, but the days of the one-page résumé have gone the way of the buggy whip. According to recruiting expert Jon Lewis:

> Every résumé is stronger when it is results based, so if you're showing that you raised your department's sales by a certain percentage over a period of time to show off your sales and marketing skills—important for a sales and marketing position—the ATS software will likely notice. Also keep in mind if a position calls for someone with five years' experience and you have three, the software will pass you over, so make sure you fit the requirement as closely as possible and remain realistic about the job hunt. Software or not, the HR director won't talk to you if you're

applying for a job with too few years under your belt. The goal is to get in front of the decision maker as quickly and seamlessly as possible.

Macy tells her students and new job seekers in general that if they are serious about setting themselves apart, type in "Free SEO webinar" in Google or Bing and attend a session. "It's an hour of your life that will inform you immensely on how this stuff is working," she says. "You don't need to be a programmer, but you need to understand that your résumé will wind up in a black hole every time unless you start getting a clue and get yourself educated on how this stuff works."

You know how it is: sometimes, when all else fails, take a class. Some of Macy's students at UCLA initially say to her, "I think Twitter is stupid and my kids are on Facebook and I'm not sure if I should be there and I tried LinkedIn but nothing happened and I don't even know what you're talking about when you say Pinterest, Instagram, Foursquare, and Tumblr. It's all Greek to me."

Fortunately Macy is happy to report that within a short period the forty- and fiftysomethings start getting "a clue," partially because they are not getting work without embracing the web-enabled world. Even so, they go to seminars, attend online webinars, attend networking events, and start hearing from others who are using LinkedIn. Then they come to her and say, "I've done all this and my phone still isn't ringing!"

This comment hit me like a ton of bricks. *This is me. I've made it to the starting line!* After all I learned, I've just scratched the surface. I sighed.

Macy looked at me and said, "You just don't walk away now and say, 'Well, I'm going to go play golf and hope somebody finds me.' You have to work it." One way of working it is to join and be active in groups and get involved in discussions within your industry.

This links back to building a robust personal brand. Groups are useful for their discussion boards, news postings, and networking—asking questions, giving advice, and finding answers. What's more, recruiters search groups for new talent. Professional recruiter Jon Lewis is a self-professed LinkedIn junkie who encourages new job seekers to spend at least an hour a day grooming their LinkedIn presence, which includes group work. "The point here is you're engaging with like-minded professionals who are getting to like and trust you. You are establishing yourself as an expert, and people will start to recognize you and say, 'Oh yeah, he knows what he's talking about—he's very intelligent.' Ninety-five percent of the time those same people will log on to your website or blog to learn more about you. You are making your personal brand relevant and current. You're showing a potential employer your value."

Lewis emphasizes that the name of the game is to outcompete the competition. He likens it to being a business owner—you have to know what and who you're up against in order to stay ahead. "As a tenured job seeker, you are competing with twenty-seven-year-olds who are using Pinterest and Instagram to build their résumés with embedded video—and they are getting the jobs," he says. He knows this because he runs a search company called www.icacreative.com that focuses on placing highly trained designers who produce digital effects for broadcast and cable television.

There are some beautiful résumés out there. Now, does everybody have to have a *living résumé* on Pinterest? No. But keep in mind you're competing with digital natives, people who are comfortable in this social media landscape. This is how they communicate. Their résumés are interesting, creative, and totally social in terms of how to find cool jobs, how to apply for them, and how to talk to people. I'm not suggesting we all have to turn into twenty-seven-year-olds, but you have to know what's going on in the world.

● **WHAT IS A LIVING** résumé anyway? A living resume is multimedia in nature featuring embedded photos, stylized graphic designs, and in some cases includes video clips.

By the time my youngest daughter graduates high school, she'll probably be sending holograms to apply for jobs, I thought. The deadline I had set to land a new job was slowly, then quickly and more rapidly sliding away. It went from a month's time at most to my growing acceptance that it could take six months to land a new position. With that in mind, my search would put me into the month of September, maybe October. That was only a few months away.

Impossible.

I found myself becoming more depressed for longer stints. I became more isolated too, even though I was spending more time around the kids on a daily basis. The key word was *around*. I wasn't spending time *with* them. I couldn't bring myself to just hang out and "take it easy." It wasn't an easy time, and my personality wasn't prone to go with the flow even on a good day. At this point I could have walked into a room of people celebrating my birthday, and I would have felt alone. It was pathetic—on different levels. It was pathetic on a personal level because I was failing in what I set out to do: land a job quickly. It was pathetic because I always thought of myself as a person of value, and that now felt totally

meaningless in this new job-hunting and networking sphere—
in any sphere for that matter. In the beginning of my search, I
trawled job postings that matched my skills and title. I used free
job boards such as Indeed, Monster, and Simply Hired. I used
paid sites like TheLadders and PRCrossing, to no avail. In my case
vice president positions were few and far between. I was finding
in this job climate that companies were hiring from within at that
executive level.

I would best describe myself as a generalist, something coveted during my career, especially if you wanted to run your own
agency like I did for more than a decade. However, the tide has
shifted to a job market favoring workers who specialize. For example, I went cross-eyed looking at job posts from companies
searching for web developers who needed to have knowledge
of AS/400 web development tools and utilities, Apache Server,
RPGsp, SQL, HTML, CSS, XML/JSON, JavaScript, Ajax, and
ActionScript; or companies looking for an operations person
with specific skills to run a small financial services company that
were not immediately tied to revenue generation; or a marketing person who specialized exclusively in digital engagement and
data mining; or someone who needed to be head of "human experience" in his little area of expertise or something like that—
and on and on, with a very long list of skills along with history
and education and certifications. Where does this leave me?
Feeling hopeless, behind the times, underqualified, overqualified,
looking to go back to school, to crawl under the school or, better
yet, back to the womb.

Millions of people are experiencing this same paradox. My
friend Marc Fischer, a corporate operations generalist, describes it
this way:

My circumstance reminds me of a story the prolific sports columnist and former HBO boxing analyst Larry Merchant wrote about Mike Tyson. In the story he refers to Iron Mike as being a "mile wide and an inch deep." He was right. Tyson can come out in the first round and in a flurry, hit and punch a ton, but once you brought him past that point he was not a boxer, he had no skills beyond that. And that's what it was starting to look like I was. I was starting to look like Mike Tyson, a mile wide and an inch deep.

I don't want that. I want to be narrow and deep, but there was no way I was going to be that. At my age I'm not going back to school to get a degree or something like that. I had to figure out a way to package myself and make it look like I was more attractive to a firm that needed what I had to offer because I have a lot to offer.

Perfect. Metaphorically speaking I was more than an inch deep in every sense of the allegory, but I also knew I needed to start talking to firms who were looking for people like me who could cover a wide range of topics, spread themselves out like on octopus when necessary, think strategically, act tactically, and be a good cultural fit. All of these positive attributes described me, but *nobody* was listening. Or so I thought. Up until now who was I talking to? The answer scared me.

Job Search Business Plan

Spruced up résumé? Check. Online presence? Check. Ready to rock? Not so fast. These days, it's not about what you want for your next job. Landing your next job is all about the hiring manager and what he or she wants. Sounds simple enough, but it wasn't long ago when it was the other way around.

So what does this all mean? It means the job seekers, you and me, need to develop a strategy for the job search, and we need to position ourselves in ways that encourage the hiring manager to say, "Dwain's a good fit for this job I am looking to fill and I want to talk to him." It's a counterintuitive mind-set, because when we lose our jobs it's all about us, it's all about what we want to do next. But even though our skills are transferable and we think we can do something different, in the hiring manager's eyes it's not about what we can do. For the job seeker, meanwhile, it's about what you can get—can you get that job?

"My advice—take what you can get!" Mika says. Mika experienced a public and painful fall from grace when she was fired at the age of forty-three at the top of her game at CBS. Getting back in the game was a monumental struggle, even for a fighter like Mika.

"This is a brutal market, the likes of which we've never seen before. You have to get your foot in the door any way you can and then get your value back." She is blunt about the future. "You have to stop sitting around thinking you're going to get what you had, because you're not! Far from it." Here's what she told me she had to do:

> I went back into news and took a job I would have laughed at fifteen years ago. You have to reset your standards and rebuild them to get your value back. It's a long process. And once you get your arms around it, things start to move—slowly, and you have to think that what you have is better than nothing. It's a total reset of everything you ever dreamed of. I think a lot of people when they get fired are in shock and they go

through this high that happens when you first get let go. You start thinking, "Great, I'll get something better, I'll finally get out of that horrible place." And then in a couple of months that high drops to a very, very deep low!

Mika's comments reinforce the fact that finding opportunities to sell yourself to a potential company takes a strategic plan, much like a business plan you might use to start your own company. You need to put yourself into a situation where you are the candidate of choice, and you need to be able to articulate that to yourself and to the potential hiring manager. As my friend Paul Stuhlman, the career coach, puts it, I need to develop a clear, focused strategy to my search. I need to appreciate the importance of the market realities, and, because this is all new to me, I'm not exactly sure what that all means. Stuhlman breaks it to me that one of the realities is that the average job search in this market is taking a year or more to complete. *This guy's too real for me*, I start thinking. As if that weren't bad enough, he follows up by saying it's actually going to take as long as it takes even if you don't want to hear that—and by the way, even if you fear that you can't relocate, you're overweight, too old, your skills are outdated, you have bad breath, and any number of things working against you, you have to go into this battle thinking there is a solution and that you *will* find work. Stuhlman says to me very slowly, "You cannot accept that despair is your destiny."

Another factor working against today's job seeker in this hyper-competitive job market is that the hiring manager almost always gravitates toward the employed applicant. Yes, being unemployed is like walking into the high school prom with your fly down. You get noticed, and not for the right reason. Even in a market teeming with competent, overqualified unemployed people, hiring managers still tend to prefer the candidate who has a job. To illustrate how prevalent this practice is, during the worst of the crash around mid-2009, some US companies placed ads on their recruiting website noting that *no* unemployed candidates would be considered for a job.

The truth is, the unemployed candidate is always the underdog in any job market. But why does the typical hiring manager still think like this? "The answer is the hiring manager asks, 'Well, what's wrong with Dwain, why is he out of work?' That's in his head. Unfortunately it's human nature to go negative first," says Peter Dubner, a veteran executive career coach and former senior vice president and chief marketing officer for GE Real Estate.

> Personally, I think it's pretty outdated thinking. That kind of thinking dates back to the 1970s before mass restructurings were common, before the whole trend in outsourcing—before the term *position elimination* was even coined. Don't get me wrong; I understand it, I get it. But the question is, is the person unemployed because she isn't good at her work or rubs her manager the wrong way—or was her job eliminated because it was sent to Asia? Underneath it all there is a seed of doubt that follows an unemployed person. It's outdated thinking.

Dubner goes on to say that if companies were smart, they would see that it's in their best interest to hire these highly trained and experienced people who have found themselves unemployed because of the economic crisis we're living through. "How often do you have to give an unemployed person a sign-on bonus? Not often," he says. "You don't have to entice a jobless person to leave anywhere. The company can still bring the new employee on in the range at or below what they would pay an employed person who was leaving a company. It's a win-win, but I don't think companies are looking at this right now and are missing out on great opportunities to hire superstars at a discount."

Head Games

The key to keeping sane in the post–Great Recession economy is to look at your search in terms of running a marathon rather than a forty-yard dash—that is, to understand that it is both a physical challenge and a colossal mental contest. In one of his blogs, marathoner, best-selling author, and business owner Harvey Mackay said it best: "Your body does not want you to run a marathon. Your mind must make you do it. Therefore, you have to develop a rationale so powerful, a determination so strong that it will enable your mind to overcome the vigorous protests of your body." I think this is the strategy job seekers need to incorporate to confront those days when we feel like giving up on our search, to develop a rationale so powerful that nearly all negative self-talk ceases to exist, allowing us to overcome the struggle that is so intense it feels partly physical in nature, when in reality 90 percent of conducting a successful job search comes down to managing what many career counselors refer to as your *inner game*.

Successfully managing your inner game greatly impacts the success of your search, according to Stuhlman and Dubner. They say your inner game may be the least tangible aspect of a job search, compared to market realities and actual search execution. Stuhlman and Dubner developed a website called www .jobsearchdx.com, a first-of-its-kind online job search diagnostics tool where job seekers can identify what is required to improve their search during times of transition—all based on their own unique situation and objectives. I took twenty minutes to complete the diagnostics, where I answered a series of in-depth questions to help me understand the unique characteristics of who I was and what my search was about. The diagnostic evaluated what was working well for me, what was not, and, more important, what I should change to be more successful. I found the information invaluable. I encourage anyone who can't afford to work with a career coach to spend the nominal fee and get tested. What you don't know can hurt you when it comes to looking for a job, and this tool will put you light years ahead in your search.

The diagnostic covered all facets of the search process. Many factors applied to search execution, the obvious ones being LinkedIn, networking, recruiters, interviewing, negotiating, search management, and how to measure your progress—such as how many hours a week you put into the search, how you spend those hours searching, and how many interviews you land through networking. The idea is to measure results.

Stuhlman tells me that mastering the inner game leads to direct improvement in one's job search performance, particularly in the all-important areas of interviewing and networking. It's sort of like strengthening your mental and emotional job search fitness program, he says, the way you would manage other aspects of your life. Stuhlman and Dubner have come up with the following five factors that comprise our inner game. Understanding these principles can help rein in some of our anxiety surrounding the job search.

Drivers—your motivation, the desire to succeed, and the effort you are willing to invest in your search

Paradigms—your underlying beliefs about the job search process that play a pivotal role in how you execute

Adapters—your willingness and ability to manage change and embrace new ideas

Attitudes—the degree to which a positive approach influences your search

Habits—the constructive routines you develop that support your search efforts

"How do you think about yourself?" Stuhlman asks me. "What's going on inside your head? How will your handling this search affect you, and what are you going through with your family? When your spouse says to you, 'Hey Dwain, did you schedule any interviews today,' what have you been doing?' How do you handle that? Does it stress you out?"

Have you had any interviews today? A chill ran down my spine when he brought up the scenario of my wife "hypothetically" asking that question. It's a perfectly fair question, but one loaded with insecurity-inducing trauma to any unemployed soul. A good friend of mine who unexpectedly lost his job in Manhattan as a senior asset manager was closing in on a year out of work. He became so paralyzed by fear when he was asked how his search was going that he stopped talking to many of his friends and family members. "My dad even made a conscious effort to stop calling because every time he called he would say, 'So how's it going? Any job prospects?' and I would tell him, 'I'll let you know when I have something. I'll call you back.' Now I find myself not even calling him because I have nothing to say. There's that much denial and fear of failure I'm dealing with," he tells me with a wince of pain in his face.

My friend will never forget when he got the ax—December 7, 2011, Pearl Harbor Day. Bombs away! His boss flew in from the West Coast to accompany him for what was supposed to be a series of client meetings. Instead, my friend was called into a conference room and served the bad news. "I'm forty-nine. I was dumbfounded" he recalls. "Sure, it's happening everywhere. There are firms laying off their higher-priced talent and bringing in people for cheaper, so it's a natural way for producing more cost-efficient returns, I guess. But when it happens to you, you don't really care about the rationale behind the happy jack decision."

On that day the company cut a hundred people from its workforce, further decimating financial industry jobs in New York, where thousands had already been fired over the past two years in the wake of the economic meltdown.

Picking up the pieces has been difficult for my friend. I remind him that I'm in the same boat. He reminds me misery loves company.

"Here's another funny story about what happened to me," he says. For some reason I'm thinking this isn't going to be so funny. I brace myself. "Get this, about three months before I was laid off, my wife and I bought a new house that was twice the size of our old house, just around the corner. I had even cleared it with my boss, saying 'listen, I just want to let you know that I'm buying a new house and we haven't sold our old house.' He gives me the thumbs up and we move into the new house." I'm not laughing. "So, now I own two houses, two mortgages. It's devastating." I knew it was not going to be that kind of funny.

He tries to bring his A game to his new role as Mr. Mom but finds it a difficult adjustment from the days of managing a team of capital market analysts and experts who work with companies such as Morgan Stanley, Goldman Sachs, and Merrill Lynch, to name a few.

In his own words he describes his job loss as a "violent" experience. As of this writing he had not been on an interview since being let go, a total of eleven months. He tells me,

Initially there was shock, and sadness, and then very quickly I resorted to leaning on my faith and believing that God has a different plan for me. I have tried to enjoy the time off with my kids—forced time off I might add—and made a concerted effort to connect with the family. We've done some traveling, but overall it has been a mind-numbing experience. It has wrecked my self-esteem, which wasn't exactly high to begin with, and I have developed a lot of self-hatred as a result of this whole nightmare. I have found myself resorting to overeating to dull the pain—it has been an eye-opening experience to say the least.

He does make me laugh with this story. A month after he lost his job his wife secretly placed her American Express bill on his desk two days before it was due. "It was nuts," he says. "The bill was $7,500 for the month. She doesn't work. I think she knows by now I'm not working. I just sat there and thought to myself, 'We're never going to be able to fit all this furniture into the van when we move down by the river!'"

Taking a Personal Inventory

So how does someone like me, who's feeling vulnerable, utilize Stuhlman's advice as to taking a personal inventory or "gut check" to see where I stand in regard to launching into a productive job search? He suggests some questions I should be thinking about, like: How do I feel about being unemployed? Sucks. How do I feel about this networking stuff? Sucks. That's okay; he follows up that question by saying, "Don't be afraid if you're initial response is 'I'd rather have a root canal or well . . . it sucks.'" On the flip side he says my answer could be, "I love meeting new people, this is going to be a blast." The next question I should think about is, What's my level of confidence that I will be successful in my search? "Don't be concerned here if you think 'I am very scared and I will never be able to pull this off.' On the other hand you could be thinking, 'everything is going to be wonderful.' Everybody is different." I'm starting to see a pattern here and the pattern is—there is NO pattern! The business of searching for a job is rife with ambiguity. The last question is, how do I feel about this time in my life, the next six months to a year that it could take to land a new job? Here he goes again. "Don't be disturbed if the answer comes back this could be this is the most painful time of my life."

Stuhlman is quick to point out that for some people the search will start slowly, maybe money is not a pressing priority or there are conflicting motivators. Perhaps one or more of the following applies to you:

- You have extended severance (so you don't need a job right away).
- Your spouse wants you to "get back to work right away" (but you don't see it that way).
- You're a parent with young children who is enjoying time with them during this unplanned sabbatical.
- You're at a point where additional earnings aren't needed.

- You are so burned out from your last corporate experience that the thought of returning to another one makes you dizzy.

According to Stuhlman, it's critical you spend some time clarifying your motivations—and conflicts—or else you'll likely make limited progress. In his most professional coachspeak, he tells me,

> For some, money truly is no longer an issue, but the needs for affiliation, contribution, fulfillment and/or identity remain. This requires a more baseline rethinking of your plan and perhaps an acknowledgement that you are probably not working at "finding that job" as hard as you think you are, and consequently may not be successful. Ask yourself, on a scale of 1 to 10: "How eager am I to secure employment and what's the effort I'm willing to invest?" If your responses are not aligned, reassess your motivation . . . or your expectations.

As you can start to see, the most difficult part of the job search is the *uncertainty*. I'm starting to think Larry David is on to something with going to bed late and sleeping later! No, uncertainty is definitely the culprit for most of my misery. Am I going to have enough money to pay the mortgage? Is my severance going to last long enough for me to land my next job? How long is the search going to take me? How do I go about this? My cousin has been out of work for three years; is this going to happen to me?

When all is said and done, I see that my drive to succeed in my search and my willingness to invest the effort required is one of the most important determinants of my success. For many, the issue of motivation is straightforward; for others it's not as clear-cut. People who need to replicate their income in the near term tend to be highly motivated, and so, sufficient effort is generally not an issue. But there's often a related problem here. Inexperienced job seekers like me *don't know what they don't know* about what's involved in a successful search. When I was let go, one of the first things I thought about was how could I possibly invest more than three hours a day in this?

The answer came during a conversation I had with a good friend of Mika's, Christie Hefner; successful businesswoman, philanthropist, and former chairman and chief executive officer for Playboy Enterprises Inc. For twenty years she helped her father run his empire during some of the most successful years the brand ever experienced. I have always admired Hefner and look forward to when she appears on *Morning Joe.* "Everybody understands it's a full-time job looking for a full-time job. People have to treat it like that," Hefner says. She knows firsthand how difficult it is for people with experience to find work since the crash, especially senior-level executives. Hefner tells me that after she left Playboy the company moved its Chicago and New York offices to Los Angeles, and as a result quite a number of longtime senior employees lost their jobs. She played a role in helping a number of these former colleagues find employment, including Playboy's corporate controller, who had been looking for more than two years. Her mantra is "Don't let yourself get discouraged. It only takes one hiring person to say yes, and you're back at work." Her advice: "You have to engage in infinite networking, every circle of friends and acquaintances you have, and not just in the business world, but people you know from not-for-profit activities or religious activities or political activities—you want everyone to know that you are looking and that you're willing to talk to anybody because you never know what conversations might lead you down the path to a job."

Don't get discouraged. Engage in infinite networking. Wise words. Let's examine their impact more closely.

4

BECOME A
NETWORKING MACHINE

Rules of Thumb for Effective Networking

Although companies are starting to hire again, unlike the dark days of 2008, many employers today are still saying that they will only hire under extreme conditions. They're hardly buying paper clips, if you ask me. But 2010 started to get a little better, 2011 a little better, and 2012 and 2013 has been getting better for some people, but there are still millions of professionals stuck in what I call "the funnel effect," circling around the rim of the job market, working their way ever so slowly through the narrow stem to an eventual job opportunity.

Some economists estimate it will take until 2023 for the supply of talent in the United States to reach acceptable parity with job demand. Stands to reason, then, that until then the friendly hiring manager holds all the cards. They can be as picky as they want to be. Does the perfect candidate ever show up? Maybe, maybe not, but there is a steady stream of good talent knocking on his door allowing him to be extremely selective. That is my biggest frustration, because I can do the job and would get the job in any other market, but I may be missing one little piece—which is almost always going to be the case, and in this case it knocks me out of the running. Employers are waiting for perfection to walk through their door.

I had the opportunity to sit down with Joe Echevarria, CEO of Deloitte LLP, in his midtown Manhattan office a day before he was flying off to the 2013 World Economic Forum in Davos, Switzerland. I asked him what advice he could give jobless executives who were preparing for their next act. As a caveat, he spoke in theoretical terms, because he has been employed with Deloitte since 1978 and hasn't experienced a job interruption. His insight was invaluable for anyone looking for a strategy to jump back into the workplace as quickly as possible.

If somebody said to me today, "Joe, guess what, at Deloitte we have 50,000 people working here in the U.S. and we only need 49,999 and you're the one who's out"—what would I do? For whatever reason, something has changed in the supply and demand equation. I would have to reset, to take a different journey and recognize where I can fit into the new equation.

I'm fifty-six years old and have spent thirty-five years on the clock—in my field, there's a lot of demand for a certain level of people with my accounting background; however, there is *not* a lot of demand for CEOs. So I would ask myself, What can I do and where is there demand for my skills? For me the answer is easy. I would teach. First, I love teaching, but my practical experience in accounting also meets an important demand in academia.

Most individuals in transition prefer to think opportunistically and focus on uncovering as many opportunities as possible. Unfortunately, they commonly tend to uncover many opportunities that are not the right fit for them even though they may get some preliminary review by the employer or an initial screening. In the end they don't advance very far. So, it's incumbent when conducting a search to take a dispassionate view of the marketplace and identify the kind of position you would truly consider to be an excellent fit.

It starts with an analysis of the marketplace. Paul Stuhlman and Peter Dubner are experts in this area. Dubner walks me through a typical scenario over burgers and beer at a local brew house.

Assume somebody lives in Stamford, Connecticut, and they're absolutely unwilling to relocate. They've worked in the banking industry and they don't come from a function like human resources or communications where they could easily transfer to other industries, but they work in operations or marketing and the likelihood is quite strong that they will have to stay in that industry. So it's crucial that they identify the number of employers within that acceptable geographic range, anticipate within each one of those employers, depending on the size, how many individuals like them might have a current position.

What Dubner is saying is, if you do a little math and you take X number of employers multiplied by X number of people who have this position at any time, some portion of that number are going to turn over on an annual basis. People will resign, quit, get fired.

"For example," Dubner starts again, "let's look at the top executive in retail operations for a bank. There is only one position in each one of these banks, and if there are ten banks in this person's geographical area, hypothetically there are ten potential opportunities in his or her marketplace. Some number of those, maybe a handful, if that, will turn over in the coming year, and on top of that a certain number of those positions will be filled by an internal candidate."

He goes on to say that if 50 percent are filled by an internal candidate, then only half are going to be filled by an external candidate, which is starting to shrink the number of opportunities available, assuming he or she even uncovers these jobs in the first place. You can't take that part of the equation for granted.

You see where this word problem is going . . . the job seeker is starting to weigh: "How important is it for me to stay in Stamford? Maybe I need to think about relocation." But if the job seeker's entire family is living in Stamford, moving may not be an option. Maybe a weekend commute? How does that impact the search?

At this juncture I'm thinking maybe I should open a little hot dog franchise down by the river near my friend's soon-to-be parked van.

Joking aside, there is a very important lesson to be learned here. "The unfortunate reality is, most individuals completely overlook taking a dispassionate view of analyzing their market to try to help them understand what potential opportunities may surface in the coming months. Believe it or not, executive-level people don't do any analytical approach to their marketplace, and what compounds the problem is they tend to exaggerate how their skills are transferable to other industries when they're not," Dubner says.

The simple truth is I have to become a networking machine like some of the other candidates Stuhlman is helping. My attempts at landing a job have failed so far, and I'm starting to see the reason is I'm not totally embracing networking as if it were a life-or-death proposition. I realize that, instead of wallowing in emotions and self-doubt, I need to overcome the fear that lies in wait just below the surface. I need to step out of my comfort zone and start asking people for help.

What follows is a treasure trove of advice from a handful of women and men on what to do and what not to do when asking friends, colleagues, family members, and virtual strangers to help you land a job.

● HERE'S HOW IT'S DONE.

"If you were a networking machine, you would reach out to twenty people a week, and of those twenty people you would have ten conversations of substance, many over the phone, and of those ten conversations you would get another twenty names of people to talk to," says Dubner very matter-of-factly.

Every time you talk to someone, the goal is to get two new referrals, and so it goes. Rocket science? Of course not. Easy to do? Sort of, if you look at it as a job and treat it with the discipline it demands. Look at the advice above as the secret sauce to landing a job. It's a numbers game. Get it. Read it again—it's easy to dismiss. But it's much more than a numbers game. In this job market, both sides of your brain need to be firing. A month into trying to turn myself into a networking machine, Stuhlman came to me and, sadly, gave me a C+ for my effort.

I'm a little too "right brain," I suppose. I'm a disciplined person, but some people who start the process can develop a common side effect I call "procrastination syndrome." Every time I started to focus on making calls and following up on e-mails, my attention drifted to, say, the *New York Times* app on my iPhone or another episode of *Mad Men* on Netflix. One morning while working at my desk, my attention was drawn to a live in-studio medical show I had never seen before called *The Doctors*. Big mistake. "We'll be right back with more 'Scoop on Poop,'" one of the doctors said with a toothy smile as the show went to commercial break. You guessed it, that kind of poop. I couldn't turn away now.

After the commercial the show launched right into a segment where Dr. Travis Stork, dressed in surgical scrubs, invited several ladies from the studio audience to join him on the set. He handed each of them separate ends of a piece of white rope and, under doctor's supervision, asked that they both walk in opposite directions across the stage until they ran out of rope. There was a moment of silence when they came to stop. The length of rope sunk in. With a handsome nod Dr. Stork explained that the rope the women were holding stretched twenty-eight feet across, the same length a normal adult's intestinal tract would stretch.

Fascinating, I thought. Perspective is everything. But this bit of information was not as captivating as when Dr. Stork went into detail about the 160 different types of putrefaction-causing microbes and bacteria that live inside that rope, I mean digestive tract, one-third of which are known to produce poisons. Dr. Stork was on a roll and continued his lesson with a warm smile, explaining how the largest number of these various species of bacteria is found in the colon, and that as adults we are carrying around three and half pounds of the stuff. Then he went into something about unusable residues of food, mucus, bile, and other body wastes, encouraging the growth of just the right amount of disease-producing bacteria . . . he lost me back on the three pounds of crap stuff. I was still trying to visualize that going on in a bikini.

Enough already! Back to work. That's what procrastination will do to you . . . or at least to me.

So, let's say Echevarria does find himself out of work, which I highly doubt will be the case anytime soon—like ever. But for the sake of storytelling, let's say he decides that he wants another CEO position. Then, like anyone else, no matter how far up or down the scale, he will have to become a networking machine to make that happen. Even he knows that. The thought of Echevarria having to work as hard as I do to land a job is pure folly, so I say. I have no doubt that if Echevarria did find himself in that situation, he would give new meaning to the term *networking machine*.

I met said networking animal while researching this book. His name is Ben Blackburn, a bona fide networking Tasmanian devil who resides in the wilds of Cheshire, Connecticut. Blackburn worked for Motorola for twenty-three years as a business development and process improvement leader, until he was laid off in March of 2012. Much like me, he wound up out of a job when a new higher-up was brought in to run his department. As Blackburn tells it, his boss was looking for a *unique* set of skills he didn't have. He quips he was victim to what he refers to as the "Khmer Rouge" mentality at many corporations, where a company brings in an outsider and puts him in a senior role, and that person starts killing off anyone with legacy or knowledge regarding how the old regime operated.

I can relate. It's not unusual for new bosses to want to establish their own culture and appoint their own lieutenants. The whole culture changes, and all of sudden buzzwords get bandied about on how the company is pursuing operational efficiencies or is going to start looking at cost structures: code for "you're fired." But, as Blackburn will attest, the code words corporations use get old. It's as if they all went to the same management seminars and learned to use the same terms.

Blackburn isn't the first to point out that companies have taken advantage of the downturn in the economy and latched onto the Machiavellian mentality where loyalty means nothing. I'm not alone in thinking that many employers are not hiring because they want to keep their profits up and pensions and health benefits costs down. I agree with him that companies are taking advantage of economic and political uncertainty. However, there has always been uncertainty in corporate America, and companies like Xerox, IBM, and Coca Cola have always been able to manage. They know what to do. They do what they do best, and that is bankroll lots of money. "It's un-American and I really mean that," says social media marketing expert Beverly Macy. "These big employers need to start hiring people—they have plenty of money to hire. They are sitting on it, and I think it's a disgrace."

Networking—and the Four-Fives Rule

"Networking saved my life," Blackburn proclaims. "However, when I first started learning how to do it I thought it wasn't for me."

Blackburn likes to point out how young he looks at fifty-three. I think, like most of us around his age, we tell ourselves that in order to overcome the fact that, whether we like it or not, our age works against us.

When Blackburn started out, he likes to say that he went into his "networking career" after losing his real career as a self-described introvert. Not the best personality trait to bring to the networking job. But, being one of the most disciplined people I have ever met, I was not surprised to hear how quickly he landed his next position.

He was also a student of the Paul Stuhlman school of networking and job placement, and, as such, he learned the first step of a successful search is to take a look at the overall geographic area you are trying to stay in and gain a clear understanding of how many opportunities exist in the market at that point in time. I was learning that it was paramount to have a clear focus on the market realities and the qualifications that match that focus and to make sure there was a sufficient number of potential opportunities in the market.

I pick up the phone and call Blackburn to see whether I can get my networking grade up to a B. I learn that he put his own spin on what Stuhlman taught him. "I was very disciplined with my search and implemented my own program that I called the four-fives rule," he says. He made sure that every day he talked to at least five people by initiating at least five communication streams either via e-mail or phone, responded to five job opportunities he found online or through other sources like headhunters, and then sent out five résumés each day. His goal was to complete at least twenty action steps; otherwise he felt like he had a bad day. Sometimes he sent out ten e-mails and called seven people but by the end of the day met his goal. Twenty was the magic number. He took the weekends off. Most weekdays he called it quits by 4:30 p.m. because of sheer exhaustion, but as he continued hitting his goal on a daily basis he became more fired up by the challenge.

Once again LinkedIn came to the rescue. His LinkedIn account was the original talent pool he called upon. At the time he lost his job, he had fewer than four hundred contacts. He systematically went through the names and identified those who came even close to matching his skill set and took note of what companies they worked for. He looked for people who had the best potential to make an introduction to their company. For example, he found a woman who worked for Samsung, a competitor of Motorola, and called her and asked whether there were any current opportunities in his area of expertise at the company. Sometimes he would send a one-page brief on his background or a full-blown résumé. He would then send a note to the hiring manager if it were appropriate or whoever internally made sense, perhaps an internal talent scout. Guess what happened? Within a short period of time he probably talked to more than 150 people just based on his LinkedIn profile alone.

"I must say I got over my shyness real quick," he says with a chuckle. "I would just call up somebody and say, 'Hey Tom, I haven't talked to you in ten years, but I was just wondering if you could help me out.' I was blown away how open people were and how willing they were to help. I think a lot of people are going through this themselves or know someone close to them who is suffering, and they want to pay it forward. I think people generally want to help you if they can."

In addition to working his four-fives system, he spent a few hours each week searching online job boards and submitting résumés there as well. Blackburn became a networking guru. He doubled down on networking, and it paid off. In less than four months he landed his dream job leading a new channel marketing initiative for the key accounts division of Essilor, a leading provider of eyeglass lenses.

How to Conduct a Network Meeting

Although I know a lot of people, some in very high places, the day-to-day grind of networking didn't come as naturally to me as it did for Blackburn. I started working at it more, setting up a matrix of twenty calls a week, twenty e-mail outreaches and setting up meetings. I was becoming a madman with the networking piece. I was getting very busy and learning a lot. The advice was paying off. The question that dawned on me was, how does one conduct a productive meeting once you get the person you networked with to meet for lunch or coffee? There must be a right and wrong way to conduct a meeting to yield the best results.

In the past, when I met someone I thought could help me, I would say something like, "Hey Tom, if you hear of a job please let me know." If it were a rich friend who owned a business, or two, I would ask about any openings that came close to matching my skills. Reality check: your friends won't know of any jobs for you. All you've done is make them uncomfortable. What are the odds of a friend stepping up and saying, "Great, can you start tomorrow, and how about I pay you $250K." Ridiculous.

I needed to develop a script in my head. Just as I needed a strategic plan to conduct a search like Blackburn's four-fives rule, I needed a sales plan to lean on when I finally approached a person who could possibly offer me a job or steer me to a person who could make things happen.

"When you do connect with somebody, the first thing you need to strive for is to set up a time to meet in person, such as meet over coffee at a Starbucks," says Stuhlman. "Don't try to get the whole networking thing going over the phone, unless of course the person is out of state or something like that. Use the phone to simply set up a meeting locally."

This should be a short, uncomplicated call. Your goal is to meet in person. One way to dive in, Stuhlman says, is to say something like this: "Rick, do you have a few minutes to meet close to work over coffee? I would love to get your thoughts and perspective on my search, and I have no expectations that you know of a job for me, but I think you could help me make some inroads. Can you meet a week from tomorrow at 11 o'clock?"

When you land the meeting, you need to be prepared. You have to think, *I have twenty minutes with him at Starbucks. What do I want to get out of it?* You have to resist the question that most job seekers want to ask: "Hey Rick, do you have a job for me?" You just can't do that. Instead, it comes down to what are the questions you can ask that won't put your friend on the spot or make him feel uncomfortable responding to. You also have to keep in mind that you only have approximately twenty minutes of their time, so you can't ask a question that's going to take eighteen minutes to answer. On the surface this sounds pretty easy, but it's not, because it means you have to have a prepared script in your head. You can't just go out and wing it if you want to come away with results.

His responses need to give you some insight that could be helpful in your search; for example, a couple of names at the end of some of his responses like "You need to talk to Mark, Mary

Smith, and Simon. E-mail them tomorrow. I'll give you their contact information and give them a heads-up that you're reaching out." Dubner says to always keep my eye on the prize: at least two names from everybody I talk to. Good, solid names.

This advice is critical for success. You're sitting at Starbucks on Melrose in Los Angeles, starting some small talk with a friend of a friend who is nice enough to meet with you. You want to confirm with him that he still has twenty minutes to talk. After that, you go into your one-minute elevator pitch. How you communicate to the person you're meeting with who you are professionally is very important. You need to cover what your career has been all about, what you're best at; this is the nature of your search, so as you're wrapping that up you want to say something like, "Again, I have no expectations that you will be able to get me a job, but you might have some thoughts or perspectives that could be beneficial to me." The majority of the time this will open the door for him to say something like, "You need to talk to these three people, etc. . . . " In that case you're off and running. But sometimes he sits there thinking, *Gee I don't know of any jobs for you, but if I hear of any I'll let you know. Can I leave now?* That's where you need to come in and use some lateral thinking. One angle to take is to say, "Here are some of the recruiters I know of in my field. Am I overlooking anybody you may know about?" That's another great opportunity for him to step in, and most of the time he will have a suggestion. A second question could be, "Do you know of any other communication executives who are in a period of transition in the last several months or who have landed?" In the perfect scenario he introduces you to another executive who landed a job a month ago, and that person could have been out of work for nine months. The majority of the time that person will be able to turn you on to all kinds of contacts and will cut to the chase as to who was helpful and who wasn't with their search. Also ask to be referred to jobs he passed on or didn't make the cut for.

You look up at the clock and twenty minutes are gone, and your new friend has just given you a couple of good recruiters and at least two or three great contacts to network with, all for the price of a cup of coffee. Thank him for his time and while saying goodbye, ask him what the winning lotto numbers are for Friday night's drawing. Make sure to offer yourself as a future resource to call upon should you be in a position to help his career down the line. It's important to provide value as well as seek help.

Again, this exchange sounds easy on paper, but in practice most people are terrible at it, at least when starting out. Like I said, if you go in winging it, at least when starting out, you will fail. I called Stuhlman to let him know how I'm progressing. "I hear people say to me every day, 'I have great contacts, but I just don't work them, or call them,'" Stuhlman tells me. "Join the club, everybody does this. You know how common this is? Oh, I have contacts, but I haven't called these people. I'm unemployed, I need a job, I need money, and I have contacts, and I know I really should talk to these people, but I'm not talking to them. What's holding me back?"

The answer is, a combination of things. It could be that you feel embarrassed or are paralyzed by the fear of failure that the conversation won't go well. You're inner critic is saying, *I'm sort of hopeful that Joe will be helpful, but I'm afraid he won't turn out to be helpful after all*. I think a lot of it boils down to this: I'm out of work, I'm uncomfortable, it feels awkward asking for help, I don't like to ask for help, I like to give help. Stuhlman's advice on that: "Look at it like this: YOU ARE ON A NETWORKING SABBATICAL. Get over it and get on with it!"

Every person is different, and every job search is different for the individual. Some people are very introverted, and reaching out to other people is very difficult, even painful. I'm an extrovert if you haven't noticed, and it's still painful for me at times to pick up the phone. I think the activity of networking is an art, not a science. It wreaks havoc with that little voice in my head that says *you're not worth helping*. Sometimes I simply think the last thing I want to do is burden someone or interrupt their day—like looking for a job has become a crime. *He's probably thinking I'm calling him because I'm out of work and looking for a job.* Maybe I should consider the reaction might be, "Wow, it's Dwain calling, it would be nice to catch up with him and see what he's up to."

IT'S ALL A HEAD GAME.

Preparing for "Courtesy" Interviews

There are several kinds of interviews. There's the traditional job interview, which I need more of. There's the exploratory interview. Then there is the dreaded courtesy interview. I say dreaded because these interviews are doomed from the start, but you usually don't know it until it's too late. You think you're going on a traditional interview with a 50–50 chance of landing a job. It's all an illusion. These interviews are set up by friends, colleagues, or family members with someone who is usually very close to them who, as a *favor to them*, is willing to meet with said job seeker—in this case, that's me. In essence the interviewer you're about to meet with is doing your friend a favor in return for a future favor or feels sorry for you and wants to make you feel like there's still reason to get out of bed after losing a job. You can chalk up these interviews as practice. Period. They're going nowhere. Don't get me wrong; there's nothing sinister going on here. Everyone is trying to help, sort of . . .

Early in my search I went on an interview like this with a very well-respected business consultancy firm that had a strategic communications practice built in. It was near the tip of Manhattan, taking me nearly two hours door to door. Not good. They were known for their financial communications services. I was to meet with the senior managing director about a media relations job that was coming up soon. I had been introduced to him through a highly respected crisis communications pro and former newspaper editor.

I was excited about the opportunity. I could explain to this person what I had done in my career, and we could put our heads together as to where I might fit in his practice. I felt special. I had an "in." My friend set this up, and his vouching for me added the necessary credibility for me to be given special treatment.

We shook hands and spent a few minutes on small talk. We both discovered we had daughters who played soccer, and we basked in other commonalities. It was time to transition into the interview itself, where he pulls out my résumé and asks me about my career history. Instead, he started talking about *his* career. He didn't stop. He went on and on about how much he loved his job. I'm sure any long-term job seeker can relate to this phenomenon. I have a friend who told me he once asked a well-established friend for a meeting to discuss possible job opportunities, and the guy chewed his ear off for two hours bragging about his own entre-preneurial prowess—oblivious to the man's desperate plight and

purpose for calling the meeting. He hadn't seen a paycheck in thir-
teen months.

My allotted half hour flew by. He talked for twenty-eight minutes—when he wasn't taking telephone calls. It was astonishing.
On the way to the elevator I had two minutes to give him my
elevator speech as to why he should hire me. He said he would
keep me in mind and that I should check back with HR when jobs
get posted. It was a complete waste of time. He didn't ask me one
question about my skills or why I thought I would be a good hire.

———

I've learned much about the psychological dangers surrounding
the courtesy interview. I need to treat them more like an exploratory interview where I'm more apt to keep my hopes in check.
But the courtesy interview is addictively alluring, the forbidden
fruit—like a long-lost lover you can never quite get out of your
mind.

With courtesy interviews you're going in as a "friendly," so often the psychology for the person you're meeting with is, if you're a
friend of my friend, you're a friend of mine. It's not a bad position
to be in, and many times they are conducting an active search, but
I'm meeting with them primarily as a favor to someone else.

High-profile courtesy interviews are all the more challenging.
Mika learned of the perfect job for me. I possessed all the qualifications needed—journalism and PR. She arranged the meeting. Because of Mika I was fast-tracked to the front of the line to
meet with the decision maker, the head of a high-profile media
company.

I spent several hours preparing for the interview. The more I
thought about the meeting, the more I psyched myself up. I was

convincing myself that the person I was meeting with saw something special in me; otherwise she wouldn't take the time out of her busy schedule to bother getting together. I started to visualize working for her. I was breaking all the rules of the courtesy interview. I saw myself running the communications department and traveling to distant countries as its global leader, staying in nice hotels for a change, unlike my AmeriCares days, building awareness about the company. The hamster wheel in my head was racing overtime.

I should have noticed the first red flag when I agreed to be interviewed on a Friday at 3 p.m. no less. Try to avoid at all cost taking an interview on a late Friday afternoon. Too many distractions and everyone is focused on other things—like not working and not talking to people who are not working.

I arrived early for the interview, planning to hunker down at a nearby Starbucks to review my notes. Just my luck, the coffee shop was closed because of a water main break. It was twenty-six degrees that day. I nearly froze to death trying to find another place nearby.

I arrived at reception ten minutes early and waited to be brought up to the meeting. My hope was to get twenty minutes with Mika's friend to show her why I was the best candidate for the job. I was thrilled to be on the ground floor of something big here. I was getting a crack at proving myself for a job I felt confident I could win—as long as it wasn't too late.

I felt good, relaxed and ready to go. I thought, *I am finally getting the break I need to get back to work.*

A few more minutes ticked by, and the interviewer's assistant came out and introduced himself. He was sharp and friendly. I immediately liked him. He started describing the position and what they were looking for in the global lead. He was describing me to a T. "We need somebody to build a communications plan for us, someone who is strategic. Right now there is a lot of chaos. We have four people working in the department, and they're all overworked and compensating for the lack of a department head," he said.

I could taste it!

I was on. The first thing the decision maker asked me was how I knew our mutual friend, Mika. That was an easy story to tell, so I set off explaining how we had known each other for more than twenty years dating back to my days working as head of communications for AmeriCares. She jumped in to say how much she loved Mika.

She told me to continue my story. I was getting in the zone when she slowly reached over to a dish of shelled pistachio nuts sitting in front of me on the table and meticulously picked out a few and little by little proceeded to put them, one by one, into her mouth. Not missing a beat I continued talking as I watched her chew. I could see the ground up nuts on her tongue as I kept speaking.

She looked down at her smart phone to check her Twitter feed. I was now talking to the top of her head. She looked up, gracefully smiling. I could hear myself talking.

I wrapped up that story and was about to ask her a question when she asked me another question. Her hand went for the dish of nuts. I looked over to her assistant to make sure I wasn't losing him too. His eyes darted back toward me. I had lost him as well. Damn. She was looking at her phone again. The reality was I never had a chance to "have them" in the first place.

And so it went. It felt like an eternity. But only five minutes had gone by.

More nuts.

I heard myself talking—and talking and talking. I felt like I was putting on a show but nobody was watching the performance. I finally stopped and to all our surprise started to make a puppet-like motion with my left hand as if it were now doing the talking, as I said with a smile, "Geez, I'm sure doing a lot of talking here; is it okay with you if I ask a few questions?"

It was time to hit the reset button on this interview. She finally said, "Dwain, I really wanted to meet with you because when my friend Mika said 'you must meet Dwain' for this position, I listen and will do whatever she asks. But in full disclosure we are quite advanced in our search and have two candidates that are far along in the process." Red flag number two.

My spirit was instantly deflated, but I tried not to show it. "I understand," I said. "I didn't realize you were that far along because we were sitting down today, but is there any way I can encourage you to reconsider throwing me into the mix?"

She said she would get back to me next week to see how the other candidates were faring. She shook my hand and said it was a pleasure meeting me but that she didn't want to waste any more of *my* time.

Her assistant walked me out.

It's difficult to avoid interviews like this because, unlike traditional interviews where I try to make sure a job opening still exists, it is almost impossible to ask those kinds of qualifying questions when a friend or colleague sets you up on a courtesy interview. With courtesy interviews you let your guard down. You go by assumptions that often prove to be false. It's what I would consider to be a "warm" interview.

But go you must. You never know what might transpire. There may not be an opportunity with her today, but the fact that we met and hopefully she liked me, puppet hand and all, might go a long way toward hiring me for a future position or referring me to a friend who is looking to hire. Besides, there's no networking going on sitting at home by myself. Time and again I've found that getting out and meeting people leads to something down the line.

I took the subway back to Grand Central alone with my thoughts. A blankness fell over me. My wife was texting me to ask when I would be home. Grand Central was a zoo celebrating its one-hundred-year anniversary.

Instead of heading for the train back to Connecticut, I turned on my heels and headed down Lexington and popped into a favorite Thai/Vietnamese place on Forty-Fifth. I caught the 6:07 train to Westport after dinner.

As I walked to my car from the train, I noticed about fifteen feet in front of me a man and woman walking, and I could hear them talking, something about "the PR business." I couldn't believe it; upon closer look I recognized it was the CEO of a respectable midsize PR practice in New York that I was very familiar with. In fact, this was synchronicity at its finest. Early in my career I hired his firm to help me with PR for a UK-based technology firm where I was head of corporate communications for its North American operation. Unfortunately, six months into the contract the United Kingdom pulled the plug on using outside agencies. It was an abrupt ending, and I never had a chance to speak with the CEO about it.

I called him several times to discuss the situation, but he never returned my calls. Now he was standing several feet away from me in a freezing train station parking lot.

As the woman peeled away to walk to her car I seized on the opportunity after all these years and said, "Hello is that you, Ken?" "Yes it is, hi who are you?" he asked.

I went on to introduce myself and bring him up to speed. We stood there chatting for a few minutes in the freezing cold; all the while he was very warm and open. I explained what had happened all those many years ago, and he laughed and said, "No hard feelings I guess, right?"

I laughed and wished him a great weekend. As I turned to head across the street to my car, he asked what I was up to these days. I told him that I was still in public relations but that I had recently been laid off and was looking for work.

"Send me your résumé!" he said with a smile.

It was music to my ears. I also thought if I hadn't decided to grab a quick dinner in the city that night, I would have missed meeting Ken and the potential to work for him. Synchronicity in action!

Track Your Yield

How many new names or referrals do you receive from your one-on-one networking interactions? Do you know; do you track this metric; have you ever thought about this? You've learned how important networking is and learned how to conduct a successful networking meeting, and yet most career coaches say very few job seekers even attempt to assess their effectiveness at it. Like anything else in life, if you don't measure the effectiveness of your efforts, how will you identify what improvements to make? While the thought of this may make you feel uncomfortable, it is the key to conducting an effective search.

Certainly, successful networking is much more than just numbers and names. Effective networking is about having conversations with individuals who can positively influence your search, individuals who can provide information and advice—as well as referrals to others. And yes, the *quality* of your referrals and interactions matters. But quantity matters too. The simple fact is that if your network doesn't continue to expand through additional referrals, your search will gradually diminish in effectiveness—and perhaps grind to a halt. Networking is critical to expanding reach and exposure in the market—with each additional networking contact, the probability of identifying and getting access to a new opportunity increases.

So what should your networking yield be? According to Stuhlman and Dubner, highly effective networkers average a minimum of two referrals per interaction—and those who do often report "there aren't enough hours in the day to follow up on the new contacts they are receiving." This can be a problem—but a nice problem to have. Stuhlman says if you're not currently generating many new referrals, don't be alarmed—it's common—and it can be fixed. Start by finding out where you are now by tracking this metric, and then look for ways to improve. Remember the words of management expert Peter Drucker: "what's measured improves." Metrics do matter, and knowing where you're going significantly helps beat back the fear of failure and rejection.

5

BUYERS' MARKET

Know Your Value

The good news is the Great Recession ended in June 2009, according to the independent group of economists who make up the National Bureau of Economic Research, the official body charged with dating when economic downturns begin and end. The bad news is hardly anybody seems to have gotten the message. And those who did felt little comfort hearing about it or for that matter believing it. What difference does it make? Millions of Americans are still out of work, losing homes, and uncertain where the next paycheck is coming from. Officially, the recession lasted eighteen months, starting in December 2007—for those who care to etch that date in memory—and has gone down in history as the longest and deepest downturn for the US economy since the Great Depression. Great this and Great that.

Real estate developer and owner of *US News & World Report* and the *New York Daily News* Mortimer B. Zuckerman has written extensively about the devastating toll this recession is taking on American workers and families. Bread lines and soup kitchens of the 1930s may not exist, "but 15 percent of the population in the United States isn't working full-time, and that is unprecedented for America except for the Great Depression. Sixty-eight percent of the jobs today are taken by people who are employed part-time," Zuckerman tells me.

In a powerful article he wrote for *US News and World Report* on February 28, 2013, Zuckerman reported on chilling statistics from the American Enterprise Institute and the Center for Economic and Policy Research: a worker between the ages of fifty and sixty-one unemployed for more than a year has only a 9 percent chance of finding a job in the next three months, and workers over sixty-two have only a 6 percent chance. "The recession has clearly shown that employers now think they can make do with fewer workers. Over 20 percent of companies now say that employment in their firms will not return to pre-recession levels," Zuckerman wrote. And he had more sobering news to share:

> The unemployment numbers are much worse. We have 49 million people on food stamps in America; that's 15% of the population. That's unprecedented. Food stamps are for people who can't afford to buy food. So something's going on there. Then there are the more than 11 million Americans who are collecting checks from Social Security to compensate for disability in the 5 years. There is no way that many people suffered injuries in the American business world. American business is way too smart to let that happen. It's become a substitute for unemployment because you get lifetime unemployment compensation in the form of disability and we're

going to run out of money for all these programs. So, this is something we have not seen since the 1930s.

Executive search expert Peter Bell can't remember a recession this paralyzing. "I also have friends who are totally unaffected by this because they're wage earners and out of the city and didn't really get how people could be unemployed for a year or two. That realization lagged, but I think at this point everybody understands—maybe not the reasons why and from whence this came—but everybody gets how really bad this has been."

By early 2011 mass layoffs in our country slowed down, but job growth is still feeble. There are millions of heartbreaking stories about how the crash has destroyed the American way of life. People have lost their jobs, their businesses, their sex lives have gone to pot, marriages have been torn apart, retirement savings have spiraled down the drain, people are suffering from mental anguish and depression, and many people have turned to vice and drugs for temporary relief from a long-term problem.

Combat the Psychological Ravages of Unemployment

I have become no stranger to the depressive and physiological effects of the job search. I get up in the morning and head to the computer to check e-mails to see who has responded to my plea for networking meetings and interviews. I constantly scour the Web looking for jobs, advice, and insight. If only I could shut off the negative voices in my head. I do take solace in the fact that I'm not alone and try reminding myself that I could be much worse off. My wife and I do have some money in the bank still and a roof over our heads. My parents have also been incredibly generous.

It helps to talk with other people going through unemployment, which turns out to be one of the best coping mechanisms a person can put in place. Just a few days of isolating can send me spiraling into a lengthy funk that pulls me away from what I need to do to get myself out of this mess.

Having a therapist to talk to about what to do when you're feeling really depressed should be compulsory in times like these. Dr. Barbara Lavi, clinical psychologist and author of *The Wake Up and Dream Challenge,* helps jobless professionals get a handle on their emotions so they can better optimize their efforts toward getting back in the workforce. She says being out of work for even less than three months can cause debilitating depression. Having a professional to share your feelings, thoughts, and stressors with can sometimes shave months off a job search. According to Dr. Lavi:

> Different people react differently but it's my experience that a high percentage of people who lose their job become depressed, suffer a decrease in energy level, and stop trying to find a job altogether because of a rut they fall into. They can't function to even try to put on a suit and go out and talk about their loss and hopefully get back in the workforce. It's ironic that in order to get a job you need to have your act together and look your best and do your best and if you're feeling your worst it's very hard to find your next job. It becomes a vicious cycle.

One of the best researchers exploring the link between unemployment and mental health outcomes is Arthur Goldsmith, PhD, who teaches macroeconomics at Washington and Lee University, in Lexington, Virginia. His research combines insights from economics, psychology, sociology, and history as they relate to employment, unemployment, and psychological well-being. He is not a trained psychologist, but in my opinion he has published some of the best research on how badly unemployment affects the psyche.

Goldsmith stated in a press release posted on the Washington and Lee University website that as time marches on for the unemployed, no matter how stable individuals were when they first found themselves out of work, within six months or more there is statistical evidence that people become more externally focused and start feeling helpless. He writes, "This compromised sense of self becomes hardened and is better described as a permanent scar rather than a blemish. Even when people become employed again, the adverse impact of unemployment on psychological well-being lingers."

He claimed that whether one is internally or externally focused prior to exposure to unemployment governs the extent to which joblessness affects your self-esteem: "Having an external locus can act as a coping mechanism or a way of avoiding self-blame, which protects one's sense of emotional well-being."

I have read elsewhere that the more highly educated people are, the more vulnerable they are to the psychological ravages of unemployment. This is because they tend to be more internally focused and therefore tend to attribute unemployment to personal shortcomings, which chips away at their self-worth.

I feel like Mr. Goldsmith is talking directly to me and understands the emotional roller coaster I'm living on. Dr. Lavi adds, "Healthy emotional development requires that people believe they are making strides to better themselves, thereby contributing to their family and community. The longer a person is not working, the more anxiety and self-doubt set in that influence decisions over every important life event, even securing meaningful work."

The fact that it's a buyers' market for corporations of all sizes doesn't make it any easier to keep your head about you. Companies are sitting on an ocean of qualified résumés and job applications. This gives them the added luxury to take their time in choosing the right person, whatever the "right person" means today. It's like shooting fish in a barrel: companies don't have to pay a premium for top talent and can keep wages low, depending on the level they are hiring for. This makes it risky for job seekers to be picky about what comes along, especially if you have been out of work for more than a year. Let's face it; at that point, whether you like it or not, you have a bull's-eye on your back flashing *Bad Apple* in red neon. In a buyers' market hiring managers don't have to offer much in incentives and don't have to conduct lengthy negotiations. If you have been out of work for a year, you're not going to spend a lot of time haggling over $2,000 extra in your paycheck. There's a line out the door of ten people who are just as qualified as you and happy to take the position for $5,000 less than what you're getting.

In a buyers' market, where supply drastically outstrips demand, interviewing becomes that much more pressurized for the job candidate. If you are coming up on a year, don't be surprised if a certain crustiness comes over you, a cynicism that forces you to fight back the feelings or delusions that the hiring manager has somehow become the Viet Cong, there to reject you and confirm why you don't belong in the workforce—ever again, for the rest your life.

In a buyers' market, you start thinking about all of your inadequacies, and all the gremlins in your head eat away at your self-confidence. It's up to me to say, *Stop! I am a good PR guy, I ran*

my own company for eleven years, was a vice president at a Fortune
500 company. I worked at a humanitarian relief organization where
I had a chance to save real lives. I have had some real success in my
career. And now I'm unemployed, and it just doesn't correlate with
how I am used to thinking about myself.

Breathe.

I will get a job or make one up. Period. It's just a matter of time,
and when it happens I will look back and say, "That wasn't such a
big deal" . . . in my dreams.

Any time an interview or a call back or anything pops up that
offers a ray of hope, I'm like a kid in a candy shop. It makes my
day. I used to get excited about the thought of saving for a Porsche
Carrera 4. Now I'm settling for an e-mail confirmation that Joe's
Widget Company received my résumé to give me that Porsche
rush. Sad. But it is these smidgeons of hope that keep me going. In
a buyers' market, every single phone call and every single conversation I have is the most important conversation in the world. But
it's really not. This is the personification of desperation.

Recruiters are the first to tell you how fat companies are getting sitting in their catbird seats. Companies have also become
much more irrational about the hiring process. "Companies expect
to meet the perfect candidate with every qualification set forth in
their job description. This is what goes through their minds, and
they expect the perfect candidate to stay with the company for a
decade. It's just flat out unrealistic," says Bell.

But this market continues to reinforce this kind of thinking,
especially in cities like Los Angeles, New York, and Chicago, where
finding great talent is easy to do. In fact, the expectations are so
out of whack that the way employers are treating job candidates is
inhumane.

Bell keeps reminding me that I need to bring my A game to every interview. I ask him why he keeps reminding people of that.

When you get into a situation like we've been in for the last five years and people lose their jobs, it goes way beyond having no income and the fear that comes with no income. This fear does seep in, but there is also a loss of identity and grief and anger that takes over. Along with this, people fall into deep depression. It's emasculating for guys. We're the hunter gatherers, and we're supposed to be out there in our identities, and when our income is taken away that affects us tremendously.

Of course there's no guarantee that once you go on the interview all will go well, no matter how well you prepare. A friend of mine who was recently downsized always does his due diligence before he goes in—upping his odds. "The problem is you know within a minute or two whether or not the interviewer is really interested in you or if they don't want you. I even find myself sitting there judging how good an interviewer they are. Due diligence only gets you so far," says Cliff Tofel, a successful medical device sales manager who made short time of getting back to work because of his persistence and networking skills. Tofel could teach a class on how to maintain a professional network and on the art of staying focused during a job search. He is one fastidious guy. But he admits, some interviews are tougher than others and can get you down if you let them. "Some hiring managers you meet don't give you a chance to shine. For those you have to fight your way through it. It stinks, and you just keep pushing on thinking, 'I have said the same thing four times and I just keep saying it because I know I'm saying the right thing, but the interviewer doesn't get it.' I just think, even if he hates me, I am eventually walking out that door, never to see him again—and on to the next interview."

Pivot Your Skill Set

One way to beat a buyers' market is to look at where the shortages are in the market, where they're going to be, and, to echo Joe Echevarria's point, to see whether you can pivot your skill set to meet demand. Echevarria is a big believer in thinking about your career as an evolutionary concept. He oversees more than fifty thousand audit, tax, financial advisory, and consulting professionals who cover a broad array of industries including aerospace, defense, automotive, banking, health care, media, and government sectors.

He suggests that, for some people who find themselves out of work, it might make sense to get an advanced degree that puts them in a more advantageous position to respond to today's market demand. "There is a supply shortage today in the disciplines surrounding STEM: science, technology, engineering and mathematics," says Echevarria. This opens up a huge opportunity for people inclined to those disciplines. He says people in certain high-paying professions need to start thinking about how they can use their vocation in ways they probably never thought about. "If you became an engineer, you would naturally think at the age of eighteen that an engineer would not be providing consultative engineering. They think engineering. They don't think about the consultative nature of engineering." You don't have to be too imaginative to see what Echevarria is getting at. Deloitte hires engineers who pivot their careers to fit demand.

"If you went to one of our consultants, they may have only been with the firm for ten years because they were in an industry somewhere else. If you look at the broad economy, STEM will be where the skill set deficiencies will occur in this country," says Echevarria.

He says parents should think about talking to their school-age kids about STEM curricula. "This is clearly where the shortages are going to be," Echevarria hammers home.

High-profile columnist, author, and *Huffington Post* cofounder and editor in chief Arianna Huffington agrees. While attending the 2013 World Economic Forum in Davos, Switzerland, Huffington told reporters that youth unemployment has reached crisis proportions in the United States. She directed attention to the fact that 50 percent of college graduates either can't get a job or have settled for a job that doesn't require a college degree.

Youth unemployment is exacerbated too by the fact that the unemployment rate for young workers, those under twenty-five, is typically around twice as high as the overall unemployment rate. This trend persists because young workers are new to the labor market and may be passed over in hiring decisions because of lack of experience. For those lucky enough to be employed, their lack of seniority makes them the first in the company to be laid off when the firm falls on hard times.

This is why personal branding strategist Stephanie Nelson says college grads have to be ready to jump at any opportunity they can get, no matter how big or small. "I tell students all the time that they need to find an internship, even if it's unpaid; suck it up and get the experience and learn about what you want to do so you're not going into the workforce blind." She also tells young people to be prepared to fight an uphill battle every step of the way. "Recent grads need to know that they are going to be up against people who are much older and more experienced, so they have to have something that they can compete with them on, and internships and real-world experiences are what will give them the ability to rise to the top more quickly."

Donny Deutsch, entrepreneur, TV personality, and chairman of namesake multibillion-dollar advertising agency Deutsch Inc., argues that there are jobs out there for young people just starting out, and aggressiveness wins the game. He tells people who are starting their careers, "There are businesses that are doing well and there are businesses that are not doing well out there, and you've got to put down the newspaper, push back from the Internet, and be the creative person who just doesn't send out that résumé, but rather target the right hiring manager and job and do what he calls 'ego massage' the person you're writing to."

His advice: find out the name of the person you're writing to, say at Morgan Stanley, and reference the last three deals she has worked and tell her you've been following her career. Tell her that you loved the way she structured that last deal you read about. "Really customize the way you reach out to people and play to their egos. That's what people respond to," Deutsch says with enthusiastic flair.

"I get a hundred letters a day that say I'm interested in a career in advertising but somebody that says, 'I heard you on TV this morning saying this and it really moved me and I loved that ad you did seventeen years ago'—that's somebody who is paying attention to me and I'm going to pay attention to them!"

Deutsch is right. I know because I subscribe to his approach, and it has served me well over the years, yet few people make the effort to go that extra mile. In today's flooded job market, it is a no-brainer to take his advice to think creatively and knock on doors.

Ironically, New York fashion designer and entrepreneur Michelle Smith has found it difficult to find good interns or even hire younger workers, including recent grads, who have the fire in the belly to work hard and learn a business from the ground up. She struggles to fill positions at her design company, Milly, an iconic youthful brand known for exquisite prints and colors and a favorite of celebrities worldwide, including Gwyneth Paltrow, Victoria Beckham, Beyoncé, and Thandie Newton. Milly is a hot brand, and the collection is sold at fine specialty and department stores in the United States and abroad, including Bergdorf Goodman, Neiman Marcus, Saks Fifth Avenue, Harrods, and Takashimaya.

> I find the millennial generation overall disappointing, in terms of work ethic. Even the interns don't want to do their own FedExes. They all seem to have this sense of entitlement. My company is an entrepreneurial environment, and I'm looking for people I can hire that are talented. Maybe it's early in their career, and I want to find someone who I know can learn and grow with me. I'm looking for that person who has a sense of loyalty like I did when I was starting out. It's really difficult to find today, especially with this younger generation.

Like any competitive employer, Smith is looking for employees who will stay with her so that she can grow them into productive team members. She says she is willing to invest in them, and if they're talented but lacking in certain skills, she will pay for them to take classes at a local college. "The way I look at it, I'm willing to make investments in them because hopefully they will return the favor one day."

Maybe paying your dues when starting out is a thing of the past. Smith says she's starting to think so. She says the millennial generation lacks an understanding of what that means before they run off and change the world. In Smith's case, she knew at an early age fashion was a calling, and she earned an art scholarship to study fashion and followed her passion to New York's Fashion Institute of Technology. She worked at the Hermès boutique in New York City to pay for her schooling and upon graduation became the first American Hermès employee to intern at the legendary fashion house in Paris. She continued her studies and interned with three other top fashion design companies before returning to New York, where Milly was born. Smith tells me,

Kids aren't interning like that as much today, partly because *Project Runway* and a lot of these fashion TV shows instill in young designers the idea that they can just go to school, graduate, and launch their own fashion business. In reality, they don't know anything, and it's really important for them to work at companies like mine or other design houses to learn and make mistakes. Even if you're not going to be an entrepreneur, it's important to earn your keep serving coffee or doing administrative tasks where you learn to *do it well*, do it the best you can—because it will get noticed and if someone is on it, anticipating the next step and performing well—it will happen for them. I just see a lot of laziness with that whole generation. It's very frustrating.

Smith started her company in 2001, and it doubled every single year. "Then 2008 and 2009 hit, and those were the first few years that running the business wasn't fun for me," she says in a calm cadence. "We still managed to remain profitable through the whole debacle, but the ready-to-wear sales are still just about even today as to where they were in 2008. It has been very difficult to grow it back."

I ask her if she has advice for professional senior-level professionals who are trying to get back in the workforce.

> I think experienced men and women who are looking for a job now need to think about being willing to take a pay cut to get their foot back in the door and prove themselves again. If they really are a performer and an asset, they will be recognized and rewarded, and they will earn their way back. It's really that hard and competitive out there right now—but talent is talent and you can't make that up.

Smith puts her money where her mouth is. Two years ago she hired a seasoned professional to launch a new accessories business for Milly. The new leader had formerly been the president of a large international accessories company and was willing to take a step down in title and pay to work with Smith, who says it has worked out beautifully. "I think she liked the idea of working in my entrepreneurial environment, and I think she enjoys the challenge of launching a business." Smith's company is also benefiting in other ways as a result of the arrangement. "She's proven to be a great example for some of my younger staff, someone to look up to. She's a great role model for some of the younger people in my office, and so it's really great having her here."

Mika introduced me to good friend, comedian, and frequent *Morning Joe* guest Susie Essman—better known to many as Susie Greene, the foul-mouthed character she plays on *Curb Your Enthusiasm.* Susie is quick to point out that in some ways the recession has helped women get ahead in the workplace. More women are going back to work because men have borne the brunt of the layoffs this time around. Having said that, Essman claims women still have to work harder than men to keep pace. To back up her theory, she tells me a story about what her physician father always used to tell her while growing up:

> "When you choose a physician, always go to the female doctor because she worked that much harder to get to where she is and therefore she's probably better," he would tell me. I think this is true. I know as a comedian I had to work that much harder in my early days as a stand-up to get to where the guys were. Women have had to work really, really hard so that in a bad economy like we have been going through over the past five years they are better able to buck up and work hard to get to where they need to be.

Essman says she is the first one to always have several backup plans in her pocket when it comes to work opportunities. Her motto is, "you can never rely on that *one thing* to happen." She makes me laugh while talking about her pet peeve. It just so happens to be one I drive my wife crazy with. "I go through this with my kids and this is the 'if only syndrome.' If only I had a boyfriend, if only I had more money, if only I had a job, and it's never that. It's always a million different things, and you always have to plan for the eventualities," she says. She speaks the truth. I'm sure once I land a job I'll be on to the next big thing that's bugging me, and if only I could fix that everything would be perfect.

"And it's hard, it's really, really hard to get past the 'if only syndrome,'" she says. "You have to be fluid. The happiest people in the world are people who can adjust to change, and the more readily you are to change and are able to change your expectations and adjust your sails to go with the way the wind blows, I think the more happy you will be in all areas of your life."

But, for some, knowing what you're worth in the workplace is tough to assess, especially when you've been out of work for eleven months and you're on the verge of a nervous breakdown. The best thing to do is to keep networking and whenever possible force yourself to go on more interviews. I know I have to stay busy, whether it's spending a couple of hours writing job query letters or going for a bike ride at the gym. As the months march along, I start to accept the fact that when I re-enter the job market I probably won't make the kind of money I made before being let go. Sometimes I think about starting my own business again, but I haven't even given that real serious consideration. There are many obstacles to getting a business off the ground in this environment. The truth is, I'm in limbo. I feel like sometimes I'm just wasting my time.

"Nothing is a waste of time—you've got to get through the day—so you have to find something to do to get you through the day, and that often entails lowering your expectations across the board," says Mika, who writes about this in her best-selling book, *Knowing Your Value*. "You're not going to be a vice president anymore; get over it! There are hundreds of thousands of people who have lost what they were. The question is, what are you today, how much can you get done in one day, how many calls can you make?

It's very, very hard to get inspired when you're unemployed. I used to waste six hours before even getting started on getting ready to get started!"

Essman says, focus on accomplishing something every day, no matter how big or small the project.

For me as a comedian and writer, I always have to go back and focus on the work. What keeps me sane is focusing on the work rather than the results. If I'm feeling anxiety and I don't have enough work to do, I have to go back and focus on writing something new and working on my craft, and that's always been what I've done.

I have to get back on that stage, even if it's for nothing, and work on my craft. That has meant more to me than the result of it. You have to avoid procrastinating on all the stupid little things that you do that make you avoid getting to where you need to go.

Leave it to a buyers' market to also ruin your birthday; that is if you're turning, say, fifty or older. You can run but you can't hide from that situation. Just as age hinders job placement progress for recent college grads, throw in some gray hair and wrinkles and see how that works out for you. Sadly, age discrimination is viewed as an acceptable bias in many of the nation's workplaces, and it has worsened in this economy. According to the Equal Employment Opportunity Commission, age bias is rampant throughout American society and business. The number of older workers filing complaints with the federal government for age discrimination has reached record levels since the recession began, rising steadily from sixteen thousand in 2006 to more than twenty-three thousand in 2011 alone.

Let's go back to the catbird seat and put ourselves in the hiring manager's shoes. There she sits with a hundred résumés on her desk with a vision of a candidate in her mind. What does the perfect candidate look like, and how many years' experience does he have? She's thinking this director-level job is going to pay between $95,000 to $110,000 with approximately seven years' or more experience, which translates to a person who is somewhere between the age of thirty-five and forty. Somehow a candidate makes it through the filtering process and walks through the door, and he's fifty-eight years old. Holy cow, she thinks to herself, he reminds me of my dad. *Can I manage my father?* she asks herself. "As I like to say, Freud has just entered the room," career coaching expert Paul Stuhlman says to me with a smile. "The fact that we've got a culture in our nation that says it's important to be young doesn't help matters either . . . "

Adman Donny Deutsch has spent his entire career in a youth-oriented business running his advertising agency, ranked among the country's top ten. His place of work has been described in magazines as "raw, edgy, primitive and home to hundreds of flip-flop clad 20-somethings using kick scooters to navigate the 143,000-square-foot maze of cubicles." Deutsch doesn't pussyfoot around when it comes to getting real about aging in the workplace.

"A lot of people have to start recognizing reality and tap into their self-awareness when it comes to their age and career path," Deutsch says. "Very often I will meet with people who are in their early fifties and lost their last job as a senior VP at an advertising agency, and I will say to them—it's OVER. Doesn't mean your life is over. It just means this chapter is over."

Is Deutsch right? I think he's mostly right, no matter how uncomfortable it is to hear. You can't fight the forces of capitalist reality. It just is. At a certain age you find yourself outside the corporate universe, and you have to start thinking like an entrepreneur. At a certain age it is very difficult to find corporate jobs. Fifty might not be the end-all, be-all demarcation line, but somewhere in that decade of life a number jumps out. I'm not yet fifty, but I realize I'm not going to be able to work my way up the corporate ladder starting at, say, fifty-five.

I put the whole fifties fiasco to business icon and media mogul Donald Trump, who tells me he's a bit of a contrarian compared to Deutsch on the subject:

> I don't think fifty means you have to go and hide or you have to go and find some kind of work that has nothing to do with what you like. To me, fifty is not necessarily the age where you have to give up the corporate world. I know a lot of great people who get jobs well beyond that age, but generally speaking companies are looking for youth. Unfortunately, that's a sad fact because a lot of great people are over fifty and offer great experience. There are opportunities out there though.

Deutsch strongly suggests that people need to start thinking about what they can do to help their own cause as they get up in middle age. He suggests thinking about starting your own business in midlife. The key is to not let a corporation tell you you've priced yourself out of the market, he says.

> You need to tap into your passions. Stop thinking about the skills and talents you have been using for twenty-five years

and dig into what your passions are and then different things start to happen. Let's say you're a guy who has been a chief marketing officer at a big package goods company, and it's very hard to get that next job. You know your skills are marketable, but maybe you've been a wine enthusiast all your life, so go out and open up a little wine shop somewhere or a digital wine selling business. Start small. It's scary, I know, but that's how you beat the market at its game relative to where you are in this stage of your life.

Bell is up front with his candidates about age discrimination. He says it's here to stay, and as a job candidate you need to embrace it as fact and move on. "We are seeing major age discrimination starting at the age of fifty and under. It's widespread. The only way to get around it is to keep turning over more and more rocks as a job seeker and look for that opportunity where you'll get hired at a company where your age is a plus-factor and not a negative. There's just no other way around it."

Trying to combat ageism on the sly can backfire miserably. You can make things worse for yourself if you withhold information from your résumé or try to hide how old you are. Bell is seeing this on a regular basis and tries to head it off every chance he gets.

I was working with a candidate who I thought was a really good match for a company, and we spoke on the phone—he said all the right things, had a great personality, and then he walked through my door for a personal meeting and I had his résumé and I'm looking at him and I'm thinking to myself— this is a different person. He left off so much information and I explained to him why that was a problem.

He said, "You never would've seen me otherwise." And I said, "You know, you're probably right but now you're taking time I don't have to spare, and how do you think the hiring manager is going to feel about you if you do that to him?—and for me, my credibility goes down the tubes.

"This isn't going anywhere," I told him. "You just can't bullshit. You need to be transparent regardless of your age. You can't get away with lying about it. Everything has to fall in place, and if you demonstratively fib on your résumé, I don't think you're going to be offered a job at that point. Now we're talking about an integrity issue, an age issue, and a guy with a lying issue. In this case it's a lie of omission. You have to deal with reality."

Reality or not, I think one of the things that surprised me the most regarding my search is the interviews where I got a sense that the hiring manager looked at me and thought to himself, *This guy has to be pushing fifty; he's just not going to fit here.* Some of these interviewers were more than ten years younger than me. It's subtle, it's age discrimination, and it bothers me. At the very least it is unfair and wrong. And, I'm a young-looking forty-nine-year-old. Other times I would look at the opportunity and think this isn't something I really want to do but maybe I should go ahead and apply to it and see if I get rejected. What gets me down the most is when people don't see my value when I meet them in person.

My friend Ben Blackburn the networking machine sums it up best: "The bottom line is at some point we all become a victim of the buyers' market."

6

WELCOME TO HELL

HR and Interviewing

HR people have to get out of the recruitment business. Simple as that. I know a lot of HR executives are going to hate me for saying that because, well, that's a big part of their job, but I think many job seekers will agree with me here. After all, if they wanted to be recruiters, they would have gone into . . . well, recruiting. I think many companies of all sizes miss out on great talent because of the emphasis and trust placed on HR people to weed out the bad and present the good candidates to those who make the hiring decisions. The problem is, I think, many of them can't tell the bad from the good. Speaking from personal experience, I have had some pretty bad luck in this area. I have sat with quite a few HR professionals who hold my life in their hands who possess neither the business sense nor the education to pass judgment on how suitable I might be for the company or the department I am interviewing to get into.

Whether I like it or not, HR is the gatekeeper to the kingdom, and as a seasoned interviewer who has been around the block a few times and who has cofounded and owned a small staffing company, I learned long ago to leapfrog the gatekeeper at all cost and go directly to the decision maker. That's taught in sales 101, and it works just as well for job seeking 101.

Understanding HR's Role—the Good and the Ugly

Most companies have HR directors interview potential candidates before passing them along to the appropriate hiring manager. They are the ones who have to vet résumés, made easier today by online application software that helps them organize and sort using keywords and other computer tricks. Of course the hiring managers want HR to find them the most qualified candidates for the position, but it doesn't add up. You can't find great people by just matching words on a résumé to words on a job description. It's elementary. Don't get me wrong; I don't think HR people are bad. In their defense they have a big role to play within a corporation. They have to be super organized and task-oriented to deal with benefits management and compensation-related duties such as payroll tracking vacation time and pay, maintaining holiday schedules, and creating policies on flexible work hours, retirement plans, and health insurance issues. They also have to monitor salary and wages and ensure that compensation remains competitive. They also play a key role in employee performance reviews, employee complaints, union negotiations, compliance, privacy issues, harassment claims, and workers' compensation inquiries. Isn't that enough to worry about? Why throw in expert talent scout as part of their job description?

"Everybody shits on HR," says my friend Adam Krumwiede, a twenty-five-year veteran media planner, who—you guessed it—is out of work and looking for a job.

> Yes, they are the gatekeepers, and as you know that's a tough role to play. There are some good HR people and there are some really crappy ones, and I would say maybe crappy ones outnumber the good ones, but if you can make a friend with some of the good ones, they can be very helpful—but they can only get you so far. On the flip side, I've seen really poor hiring managers and good HR people trying to work with them and getting completely frustrated because the hiring manager can't articulate what she's looking for.
>
> HR professionals are these middle people who don't have much authority, who pass people through and then try to take care of the details and paperwork after the fact. I feel for them.

In his now infamous 2005 article for *Fast Company* entitled "Why We Hate HR," former executive editor Keith H. Hammonds took delight in skewering the profession. It is a must-read for any job seeker or HR professional for that matter. In the article Hammonds claims HR is a disconnected entity within a corporation that is at best "a necessary evil—and at worst, a dark bureaucratic force that blindly enforces nonsensical rules, resists creativity, and impedes constructive change."

Hammonds writes, "First, HR people aren't the sharpest tacks in the box: People applying for HR positions are generally not as smart, nor as independent in their thinking, nor do they operate according to clear values. Others enter the field with good intentions, but for the wrong reasons." Hammonds's thesis leads back to the central failing of HR in general, and that is they are, for most practical purposes, neither strategic nor leaders; they don't work for the employee's benefit, lack general business acumen, and are woeful underachievers.

He also questions why, in our knowledge economy, where finding, nurturing, and developing the best talent should be the most important task of a company, does HR do such a terrible job performing that task?

You might best answer that question with a question. Would you ask your company's sales force to write press releases and come up with creative ad campaigns to run during the Super Bowl, or would you rather focus their efforts on what they're trained for—to knock on doors, open accounts, and close deals? In my opinion, a majority of large corporations in the United States are applying the nonsensical logic of the former when it comes to how they utilize their HR teams. In my book, it's the department manager's job or internal or external knowledgeable recruiter's job to find the best talent. These professionals are in the trenches and know what is most needed to move the business forward. It's their job to uncover those secret finds and entice the best talent to come on board. They walk the halls every day, know the players, and know how to duplicate those whom the company believes to be strong role models. They keep their eyes open for the right profile. They have the time to stay connected to potential employees working at competitor companies who aren't quite ready to make the jump, and they are there to scoop them up when they do become available.

Just as Krumwiede suggests, a good HR person is someone to have in your back pocket, but a good couple of recruiters who work in your field can be worth their weight in gold.

I learned that external recruiters also have challenges working with their client HR representatives. Most of the time they find themselves competing with their own client to land the perfect candidate. And, because most recruiters today work on contingency, the company saves a lot of money by filling the position internally or finding an employee on their own. Using the recruiter naturally casts a wider net but costs them nothing unless they actually hire one of their finds.

This is why, whenever possible, recruiters like to work directly with hiring managers within the companies they are working for. It cuts through the red tape, and they are able to go to the source for speedy and helpful feedback, which is the lifeblood for a successful recruiter.

"Our problem with HR is they often don't know what you do," says executive recruiter Peter Bell. Bell and his partner Barry Piatoff have been placing corporate communications and public relations executives around the country for more than two decades. "The other major problem is the lack of communication we get out of HR. When we send over résumés or a person goes in to interview, we need feedback. Communication is essential, and without it everybody's lost. We can't find the right person if we don't receive timely feedback. There are a lot of nuances, and of course we have candidates calling us for feedback as well."

Bell also believes that companies are missing out on great people because they are opening job portals to handle applicant requests to join the company. You can't speak to a live person at most companies anymore. "This all has to do with HR," Bell says. "My advice to anybody looking for a job is, if you see any daylight at all, don't deal with HR. Go right to the hiring manager if at all possible."

See what I'm talking about? Does that make me a bad guy?

A Word About Recruiters

A friend of mine told me that he learned to take the advice of a recruiter by taking the advice of his wife first. He was against the whole idea, but his wife insisted, and in the end she was the smart one. A recruiter ended up finding him a job. Personally, I have always been skeptical of using recruiters to find a job. One friend of mine who recently landed a job views recruiters as being one step above selling life insurance. I don't go that far. I really love my friend Peter Bell. And as you know he's a recruiter. I made sure that most of the good recruiters who work in my field know who I am and have my current résumé, but I also know the odds are I will grow old and die waiting for them to call with opportunities. Especially in this market where their databases are chock-full of people just like me *and younger!*

Back to my friend who smartly took his wife's advice: she believed from the very beginning that he needed to be working through a recruiter and that that was going to be the quickest way for him to get back in the game. He dismissed it. There is a curious wrinkle to the story though. My friend had finally reached the state of complete desperation and was suffering from chronic depression when he finally agreed. He started actively going after recruiters, and that sent him off in a new direction, actively searching for recruiters online, where he made a list of more than a dozen good leads. Consequently he set up meet-and-greet appointments that ran the gamut from IT recruiters, financial recruiters, marketing recruiters, and other recruiters in between. He remembers how grateful he was when some of these recruiters would see him. He realized some of the larger firms in places like Stamford, Connecticut, and Manhattan were happy to meet because, in his words, "they were in the résumé collection business to see what companies I worked for in the past where they could gain insight and gather intelligence for their own databases."

For months he stayed busy building rapport with key recruiter contacts. He touched base with them, say every three weeks, clipped an article or two, and sent it along as an icebreaker to keep the conversation going. In the end there were roughly five recruiting companies he thought were worth working with or he felt comfortable enough recommending to friends. Nothing was coming to fruition, and then one day he hit the jackpot by a total twist of fate.

His next-door neighbor, a physician and single mom with two young children, had asked him to send her his résumé. She promised to pass it along to a friend of hers who was a recruiter she ran into once in a while on the "birthday party circuit."

A few months went by, and one day she came over to the house and shared a story that eventually changed my friend's life forever. She told him that she had met an investor in a company at a birthday party, and he had a crumpled-up job description in his coat pocket. She told him, "I looked at it, and the job description and your résumé were the same person!"

She told him to be on the lookout for a call from his assistant. "Two weeks later I was hired," he said with the look of a man who had been through a lot. Because he had been through a lot. It took him fourteen months to land this job.

"All I could do was weep," he says to me. "I went out into the driveway and looked up at God in heaven and cried."

Mastering the HR Interview

The *job* of any job seeker is to bag the all-elusive interview. In Africa one is obsessed with seeing the big five (lion, African elephant, Cape buffalo, leopard, and rhino). These animals are magnificent, and spotting them is a rewarding achievement unto itself. Landing the interview is right up there, and it helps to understand, going in, the mind-set of the employer. It also helps to have a strategy in place to prepare for the meeting ahead of time. Many recruiters I speak with say the majority of people they send on interviews end up thinking they can make it up as they go. That fact amazes me, given the hours I spend mentally preparing and role-playing for the meeting.

For expert advice on acing the interview, I called Jack Mitchell, chairman and owner of high-end retail stores Mitchells/Richards/Marshs and Wilkes Bashford, a three-generation family business that operates men's and women's specialty stores in Connecticut, New York, and California. Mitchell spends a lot of his time in his Westport store, in my hometown, so I popped in for a visit. He is also the best-selling author of the highly acclaimed business books, *Hug Your Customers* and *Hug Your People*. "Hugging" is the key to his family's extraordinary success. Mitchell explains that his family's hugging metaphor brings humanity back into the workplace, not through touching but through getting to know, pay attention to, and be curious about the people they do business with and who work for them. Take it from me; shopping at Mitchells is an experience to behold. They call me by my first name, serve me cappuccino while I browse the men's section, and send me thank-you notes after the purchase, making sure I'm 100 percent satisfied with the transaction. It works. I'm a customer for life. I can't wait to get a job so I can spend more at his store. That's what hugging is all about. *Hug Your People* is Mitchell's blueprint on how to hire the right employee, motivate a workforce, and retain the very best, happiest, and most effective staff, who won't jump ship the minute a competitor across the street offers ten dollars more a week.

Mitchell himself has been recognized as one of the top ten retail visionaries of his time by the *Daily News Record*, one of the most respected retail trade publications in the country. His company brings in more than $100 million in sales.

He explains in his own words the five criteria for hiring someone he has formulated over his distinguished career. Like most great entrepreneurs, Mitchell believes that his people (customers included) are his most important asset.

Integrity and Honesty—"This doesn't mean you don't steal diamonds or clothes. It's a broader definition. I probe on this particular issue in a number of ways. I love someone who comes in my place for an interview having already read one of my books. To me trust and integrity are the most important attributes a person can have. I'm looking for that person who can learn to look the boss or their colleague in the eye and say, 'You really screwed up here.' That's the kind of person I want who will be open and candid all the time."

Positive—"Being positive is crucial, and it's more than the glass-half-full stuff. First, if you're positive, then you're successful.

You have to be happy first and hug yourself and be kind to other people. Then you become successful, and you wake up in the morning, and you're joyful, and you're grateful for your job, you're grateful for your family, grateful for your cup of coffee, grateful that you live in a nice place. Being positive is super, super important."

Competence—"You have to be able to tell me that you're a great tailor, a great salesmen, a great seamstress, and that you have leadership abilities. I can usually find this out by getting references, and I can dig in and get more details during these calls. I want the person I'm interested in hiring to encourage me to check their references and speak to those who can attest to their experience. I would even bring references with me when I'm job hunting. People who come to me and put in front of me people who recommend them—I'm not bashful, I will sometimes pick up the phone and call them."

Passion—"Passion is all about listen, learn, and grow. I want to know what an employee is reading, how are they bettering themselves, how do they grow in their position, how do they grow their career, how do they grow as a father, as a husband. If you are a tennis player, do you practice, how do you get better, do you want to get better?"

Be Nice—Enough said.

Mitchell recommends job seekers also send a handwritten note after interviews, thanking interviewers for their time and consideration. I bring up my frustrations with companies who sometimes put me through three, four, and in some cases six interviews before making a hiring decision. "I know it seems very stressful and sometimes over the top, but you have to be thinking that you are going for a career—not just a job—and it needs to be a good fit for everyone involved. We want to hire somebody. We don't do all these interviews to fire them. We celebrate when they come to work with us. We jump up and down and send them flowers. They are part of the family and we treat them as such."

Like Mitchell, Donald Trump has conducted more than just a few interviews over the years. He knows what makes people tick. He has this advice for me and other midcareer job seekers out there looking to gain an edge in the market:

> First of all, you have to keep your head up, and you have to really feel good about yourself when you walk through that door. I believe strongly that you have to dress properly. You have to look good and look sharp. I also think frankly that the résumé is very important. When I see somebody who's been on the job for a long time as opposed to somebody who you look down and every week they have a new job, that's not good.

Trump is the first to admit hiring someone good is more of an art than a science. "You never really know if the person is a winner. I've had many cases where I think somebody is good and they turn out to be total stiffs, and I think somebody who's not so good turns out to be a superstar. It's sort of like with me and *The Apprentice*. Some people we pick who we didn't expect to be that great turn out to be really terrific. You really don't know that until you throw them into the water."

Here is a valuable preinterview checklist Bell gives to every candidate he works with before sending them in for an interview with his clients. It's a simple guide of dos and don'ts that I use personally before every interview I take part in. Answer these questions thoroughly, and you're ready to go.

✓ Tell me about your experience at your last company.
✓ Why do you want to work for us?
✓ What do you know about our firm?
✓ Why did you leave your last job?
✓ Tell me about yourself. (People really blow this one. Get your story straight. Practice telling it.)

Things to Avoid

- Overexplaining why you lost your job.
- Conveying that you're not over it.
- Lacking humor, warmth, or personality.
- Not showing interest or enthusiasm.
- Inadequate research on the firm.
- Concentrating on what YOU want.
- Trying to be all things to all people.
- "Winging" the interview.
- Failing to set yourself apart.
- Failing to ask for the job.

———

I look back on how stressful interviewing was early on when I was first let go, but now I can honestly say I enjoy the give-and-take of an interview. I'm by nature a live wire who is proud of his professional accomplishments, so the performance aspect of interviewing appeals to me. I have become a brand and all that goes with it. I'm excited for the opportunity to sell myself to a hiring manager. I'm enthusiastic by nature, so just before I go into an interview I take a second to dial it back a beat. It also helps me to take a couple minutes before I go in and do a short meditation.

I still struggle with certain psychological aspects that come with the whole job-seeking process. I have been unemployed for more than ten months, and, like any job seeker, I have my good days and my bad days. I find myself hanging on every positive word I hear or read as it relates to my search. I have so much to offer an employer, but I can't seem to break through.

I still haven't gotten comfortable with the rejection that comes with this new life of mine. That's made all the harder when most of the companies I interview with I am passionate about. I want to work there. I have rarely gone on an interview where I thought, *This will suck if I have to work here. Their products suck. Their brand stinks and the people are basically Neanderthals.* Part of my meditation before going into an interview consists of visualizing working for the company. I can literally see myself in the role. By the time I show up for the interview, I feel like I am already working there.

Today I'm preparing for such an interview. If I get this job, I will take a hit in compensation—that is, from what I was making at my last company—but I want this job. It would be a boost to my ego and a super fun place to work. It just feels right.

I'm preparing for the interview—it's just me in the house, pacing and going over what to say. I walk a circle through my kitchen and into the living room and back around to the kitchen, again and again and again. I'm role-playing, and I'm thinking through what I think is going to be asked of me. I put structure to my talking points, frame my résumé in my mind just so, and organize the research I have completed on the company: I've memorized the names of the company's executive team, its board, mission statement and gone through a year's worth of press releases. I'm walking back and forth and back and forth in my little hallway, talking to myself, pretending that I'm on the interview and essentially just free-associating with nobody but Bennie the poodle we're dog-sitting for that week. Bennie sits there on the couch and watches me with his sparkly black eyes and wet little nose as I walk around the house. He is mesmerized by the whole thing, and I'm thinking how nice it is to have company to talk to. He helps me stay on point.

This is almost tragically funny. Man's best friend, right.

Show time. It was finally time to meet with the company. They were looking for a director of corporate communications to oversee their media relations, social responsibility, community relations—basically everything. It wasn't a VP-level position but it didn't matter.

I had tracked down the company's internal recruiter and sent her an e-mail hoping to convince her that I was the right person for the job and asking her to consider interviewing me for the position. She immediately responded with an e-mail that said she thought I looked like a great fit and that if my salary requirements weren't too high, she would like to have me come in for an interview.

● **ON A SUNNY DECEMBER DAY** I met with the recruiter. She was friendly and easy to talk to. She asked me the customary questions. We ticked off all the boxes concerning the résumé. I explained why I left my last employer, what sets me apart from other candidates, and why I would like to work at the company. She then explained in broad terms what they were looking for in a candidate. I could tell they weren't 100 percent clear on that front, but maybe I could help them develop the job description as we went along. I could do this job in my sleep. And that was the problem.

We were in agreement that the job aligned perfectly with my background. Too perfectly, perhaps. We were even able to come close to agreeing upon a suitable salary range for the role. Everything was going as it should. Again, all the buy signals were there. What could go wrong?

"Dwain, do you still have a few minutes to stick around?"

"Sure," I eagerly said.

"Great, I would like you to meet our VP of human resources if that's alright with you."

She left the room. I sat there for fifteen minutes reflecting on our conversation. I was excited about this opportunity. It was a great company that provided a great product, and they had major plans to expand. The door swung open and in walked Larry the HR guy. He was in his midsixties and he looked tired. He said hello, and just as quickly as he had sat down he excused himself and came back holding a bottle of ice-cold water and shut the door and sat down again.

None for me, not thirsty, thanks for offering though—already getting off to a bad start, I thought. Larry sat quietly looking down at my résumé, as if it were the first résumé he had ever seen since graduating from HR school. He looked up and began asking the same questions I had covered with the recruiter. Except the recruiter smiled and was friendly. This was starting to feel more like an inquisition.

Larry kept his nose in my résumé as I continued answering questions. I couldn't get him to come to life, and that is a rarity for me. You see, I'm a fairly animated person, and the more I tried to make him smile, the more he sat there like a stick in the mud. Unfortunately, I'm the kind of person who likes real-time feedback and reinforcement. Drives my wife crazy. That's a story for another time. For the most part this feedback serves me well. But the Larrys of the world trip me up every time.

He clearly didn't want to be conducting an interview this day. From the outset my instincts told me that this wasn't a scheduled event to begin with. As I kept talking funny thoughts started crossing in my mind. It was like I was suddenly in a movie. I pictured Larry standing up abruptly and yelling at me, "*Just leave.*" For real. I was having fun with it. My brain was multitasking a thousand miles an hour. I could feel my jaw moving but didn't hear what I was saying.

I blinked my eyes and Larry had now turned into a flesh-snacking zombie. He was missing an eye and most of his upper lip, fully exposing his yellow-looking rat-teeth. I could hear cicadas singing in the summer twilight heat as he reached his bloody hand across the conference room table to make a quick meal of my forearm.

How could this be happening? The recruiter was ready to hire me on the spot. How could I go from making such a great impression with her to striking out with him? I kept telling myself it wasn't me. Larry then asked me if I knew what the job was paying. I was quick to confirm that I had gone over the numbers with the recruiter and that I respected the range and was excited to work here.

It was finally my turn to ask some questions. I asked him if a PR agency reported into the position. Pretty basic. Somehow that stumped him. The silence was deafening as I waited for an answer. He finally said something. I was relieved. "I don't know," he said. Wasn't worth the wait after all.

He explained in broad terms what the company was looking for, and it was clear to both of us that I was more than qualified for the job. As far as I was concerned that was great. I am ready, willing, and able to do the job, *for any salary at this point*. I didn't tell him I would even clean the toilets if he let me start tomorrow, anything to get out of my house and back on the payroll somewhere.

We wrapped up the conversation, and he asked me to send over some work samples that he could go over and perhaps put in front of the hiring manager to help her decide if she wanted to interview me. I said I would oblige, but I asked for a little more detail as to what he was looking for, because "work samples" was pretty broad in scope. I hadn't had to show samples of my work for many years. We establish that he was looking for some writing samples, examples of media plans, and PowerPoint presentations.

Despite the yin and yang of the interviews I had just experienced, I was still relatively confident of my chance to interview with the hiring manager. That evening I met some friends for dinner to celebrate the Christmas season. It was December 13. Friday morning I arose early and went down to my basement office and started pulling together material to send to Larry. Being the news junkie that I am, I always have the TV on low, and I have myriad alerts set on Google and on my phone for breaking news. The first bit of news of any significance that came in that morning was that *shots* had been fired at a school in Connecticut. The AP simply stated *developing story*. Not long after, another story crossed the wire that said a school shooting had taken place in a town twenty miles from my house—a place that will forever be ingrained in our national psyche—a place called Newtown.

I immediately picked up my cell phone and called a good friend whose family I knew lived a few miles from the Sandy Hook elementary school where the tragedy was unfolding. He was packing up his briefcase to head home when he answered my call. He didn't have any more details about the shooting, but he had been in touch with his wife and his kids were accounted for.

Over the course of the day, the news poured in, and the story grew to horrific proportions. Nothing short of unspeakable evil had enveloped Newtown this day, and the entire world was brought to its knees asking simply, *why*? By the end of the day we had all heard about the deeply disturbed twenty-year-old local resident who had shot his way into the school and murdered twenty innocent first grade babies, and five school staff members. Before driving to the school, he shot his mother three times in the head—making it twenty-six dead in total, becoming the second deadliest school shooting in US history after the 2007 Virginia Tech massacre.

It was a struggle to pull together my best work to present to Larry that day. I couldn't concentrate. By 5 p.m. I finally hit the send button and off my samples went. I followed up with him the following Monday morning to learn that he was out of the office until the end of the week. I left him an e-mail and voicemail so that he would at least confirm that he received the information. I never heard from him.

By now Larry was back in the office, but the recruiter had already informed me that the hiring manager had interviewed several other candidates. All the recruiter would say is to check back later.

I sent Larry another e-mail. He never followed up. I knew he felt I was too expensive for the job, so I was hoping I could catch him and get a chance to address my salary requirements. I was livid that this man didn't have the common courtesy to, at the very least, acknowledge receipt of my material or respond to any of my messages. Weeks turned into a month, and I never heard another word from the company.

On my wife's birthday her friend came to the door with a product from the company Larry worked at.

Bam.

Like Pavlov's dog I walked into our dining room with my cell phone and speed-dialed Larry the HR guy. He picked up the phone. Wasn't expecting that. "Hello, Larry, this is Dwain Schenck. Do you remember me, the person you interviewed for the communications role, it looks like that is still open, is it not?"

"Hi Dwain, yes I remember you, you worked at Phillip Morris."

Not even close, but I got him dialed in.

"Yes, now I remember who you are."

"Thanks Larry, I am still very excited about the position you have open there," I said and then cut to the chase " . . . and wanted to ask you if perhaps I'm not being considered at this time due to a perception that I might be out of your salary range—or possibly I'm overqualified for the position, which I can assure you my qualifications could help the company immensely."

Bingo! That got to the root of the matter, after all this time.

"Well, Dwain, yes I feel you're overqualified, a bit of a heavyweight at this time, I'm afraid," he says.

"So, you feel I might be out of your price range, too?" I ask.

"Yes, that's another concern," he says. "Listen, I'm in a meeting, I would like to discuss this further next week. I will be back in the office on Thursday. Call me then."

"Perfect," I said and we hung up.

I immediately followed up with this e-mail:

Hello Larry,

Glad we connected today on the communications position. Per your suggestion, this is a reminder for us to speak again when you return to work later next week. As I mentioned, I am still excited about the role and would hate to be counted out because of any miscommunication or before we fully explore both of our requirements as to what could work for each other.

We might not be that far apart on things like salary as well. I bring much to the table, including the right amount of experience, passion, and a great attitude. I am local, my wife has a great job, which allows me to be flexible with my career, and I prefer not to take the train into Manhattan every day for my next move. I am very motivated by the brand, where the company is going in the future, and the ability to utilize and stretch my talents with a company like yours.

I look forward to your call later next week. I have attached my résumé for your convenience.

Best,
Dwain

I met with Larry one more time about the position. He was just as confused about the role as he was the first time we interviewed. As of this writing it still hasn't been filled, nearly a year after the opening first appeared on the Internet.

● **IN A WAY I WASN'T SURPRISED** at the outcome, but this one hurt. I stayed with it. I wanted and needed the job desperately, and I knew I could have made a huge contribution to the company. One of the pet peeves I notice I'm starting to develop is the lack of feedback potential employers provide. Everyone likes their phone call returned within a reasonable period of time. That isn't happening in job market 2013! And it's starting to drive me crazy.

I bring up this issue with my friend Paul Stuhlman to see what his take is on the subject, or whether he has even given it any thought.

"Welcome to the job search," he says. There's my answer. He turns the issue on its head for me. "Think about it for a second, what if your psyche didn't need any feedback? It's like, you just kept on trucking. This is a very personal experience. Wouldn't that be great if it didn't matter? We as human beings crave feedback, but it rarely comes—but what if that rolled off our backs?"

Stuhlman says that most interviewers don't give feedback because, unless you are their guy or gal, you're long gone off their radar. No offense. There's a combination of reasons why they blow you off, he says. On one hand, the HR person is thinking, *I have no interest in spending even fifteen seconds on this guy and want to go to the next e-mail.* Another reason could be he just hasn't found the time to reply. He's very busy.

Yeah, I get that, but what about the part where I'm thinking feedback will help me adjust my interviewing approach and help me land the interview faster, help me tweak my story, improve my résumé, be made aware of the fact that to my complete and utter oblivion I'm nervously kicking the side of the desk as the HR person is trying to hear my answer to his question, "If I were a tree, what kind would I be?" (Weeping willow of course . . . at this point anyway.)

"Everybody always says this, 'I just wish the employer would let me know why they didn't hire me or where I fell short—that could really help me in my next interview,'" Stuhlman says. "The reality is, even if you get feedback, it's like pabulum. It will prove to be nothing of any substance. It's not like they are going to say, 'Well you should've worn a different colored tie or you didn't handle those behavioral questions well.'"

He's right. At best, you get corporatespeak like, "We went with a different candidate who was more closely aligned with what we needed." It's legally defensible. It's not like you can then say, "Wow, that's age discrimination, I'm going to sue for this."

"Get over it. No, you're not going to get any feedback. But imagine this; imagine if the lack of feedback didn't bother you at all. Wouldn't that be nice?" Stuhlman repeats himself. I've learned that when he repeats himself I should take double stock of what he's saying.

With that advice I'm challenging myself to stand back and say, "Yes, I got turned down from that job, and it knocked the wind out of my sails for the whole week, and I was unable to do anything else, and I went to pick up my phone, and it felt like it weighed a hundred pounds, so I decided to go out and shovel snow instead."

No, the idea is to become more resilient. Being turned down for a job isn't personal. It just *feels* like it's personal because you're sitting there and they are turning you down for something you really want and need—but, hey, it's not personal—but the point is, it's really not. The market is snowed under with talented job applicants, and you have to think there will be a better fit somewhere else just around the bend.

What Stuhlman teaches people to do is get mentally tough and build up what he calls their "supreme confidence shield" to face the search, realizing that they can't control whether they receive feedback or even whether they will be hired for the job. Instead,

Paul reiterates the importance of concentrating on what you can control, and more often than not that boils down to several important intangibles that include persistence, resiliency (that word again), and optimism.

"So imagine on a scale of 1 to 10 when it comes to persistence you say, 'I'm a 10, I just don't give up. I just keep reaching out, and if you don't get back to me, Mr. HR person, it doesn't bother me. I just keep looking for the company that wants me and can leverage all of my skills.'" By the way, Stuhlman tells me nobody is ever a 10 so relax. "How about resiliency? 'I get bad news but I bounce right back up. Again, it doesn't get in my way.' Nobody is like that 100 percent of the time either," he assures the masses. "How about optimism, in the absence of anything tangible that would make me optimistic, wouldn't that be a magic elixir for people?" "Yes, it would," I say with gusto.

Stuhlman says, when he tests clients on these concepts through his and Dubner's online diagnostics program, most people score a 5 or lower.

In Search of Civility

A high-profile entertainment company based a short distance from where I live was looking for a vice president of corporate communications, and I believed I possessed the qualifications they were looking for. I had heard it was a tough place to work, very demanding and quick to fire people. A friend put me in touch with the company's internal recruiter, who said she would look at my résumé and get back to me. A few days later we reconnected, and she said she forwarded my paperwork to their outside recruiting firm on retainer to fill this position. She assured me that they would call me to discuss the opening. She added, "Just FYI, we are fortunate to have several strong candidates in the pipeline (already) whose backgrounds match the targeted qualifications, so we will be able to be extremely selective as we move forward with the search."

Thanks for that little tidbit of information, I thought. My goal of course was to speak to the hiring manager, the senior vice president of corporate communications. I asked the recruiter whether she could let me speak with him. "I know you said he was tied up, but I think I would make it worth his while if I could have five minutes with him on the phone," I told her. She said I would have to wait and speak with her external recruiting agency. So be it.

A week later I spoke with the outside recruiter, who was friendly and professional. As so often is the case, she described in more detail what the job entailed, and the more she talked, the more of a departure it was from the actual written job description. I wasn't put off by that, but in this case they were looking for somebody who had not only the prerequisite communications background but also someone who more narrowly specialized in cable programming. She said the hiring manager was very specific about wanting somebody who had several years under his belt working for a cable channel such as Discovery, FOX, or AMC. I impressed upon her that although I don't look like a slam dunk for this position, I have worked with many of the media properties the hiring manager is focused on and I have stellar national media relationships. I thought that if I could speak directly to him, he would see what a good fit I would be—that I could quickly pick up the experience he needed me to have but that the core experience he was looking for was in place.

She gracefully wrapped up the call by saying that she would get back to me in two or three weeks after the hiring manager interviewed some cable candidates they had lined up.

Nearly a month went by and I heard nothing. By then I had tracked down the hiring manager's e-mail address and debated whether to shoot him a short note of introduction. What's the worst that can happen? Isn't it always best to be proactive and show initiative? He either ignores it, or he appreciates the persistence and picks up the phone for a short conversation. I finally broke down and sent him the e-mail. I would grow old waiting for recruiters and HR people to help me. Every day was another day without a paycheck. What did they care? The e-mail was a few short sentences.

Hello

My name is Dwain Schenck. I'm told you saw my résumé. I applied for the VP of communications position.

I know you are looking for someone with cable experience, but before you make a decision on a candidate please give me five minutes to speak with you. It's common to hire a "résumé" and not a person, but I think my experience and personality will interest you. I am confident I would be the more successful candidate for the job.

Give it some thought. You have nothing to lose to take a few minutes to see why I would be a great fit for the position.

Thanks for your time and consideration.

Several days after I sent the note, the company's external recruiter called me on my cell phone. I thought she was calling to set up a few minutes to finally speak with the hiring manager as a result of my convincing note. Quite the opposite; evidently he was offended that I reached out directly to him. Instead, she was calling to say he was *going* to hire a cable guy. She went on to say that what I did was not in the company's culture. She then reminded me that I had been told I wasn't a match to begin with. What did she mean "not in the company's culture"? If anybody needed a lesson on culture, it was these recruiters.

Two weeks after having my wrist slapped, I learned in the PR trade magazines that the senior hiring manager I had offended had left the company. So what did I do? I called the recruiter and asked for his job! She said they were holding off on filling the position, but she would get back to me.

When you are lucky enough to get some feedback on an interview or if you get a chance to talk to a hiring manager these days, don't expect to be bowled over with politeness and grace. "We have found in the past couple of years that civility has disappeared," says Bell. "People aren't nice. People don't return phone calls; they just don't. A lot of this stems from the economic downturn we are in going back to 2007, 2008. There are just so many more people available for each job opening that those people doing the hiring don't have the time for all the niceties that they should have."

Bell says he and his partner tell their clients that, even if during the interview they know they're not going to hire a candidate, they shouldn't cut the meeting short and dismiss the candidate. Their advice, "be nice, show some respect—you may be sitting in that seat yourself one day."

We see this over and over and get phone calls from people we send out who say, I was there for fifteen minutes and all of a sudden the guy gets up and tells me it's over. Not only are these people leaving knowing they're not getting a job; they feel anger at the person who they interviewed with and toward the firm. It instantly translates into a negative experience for our client's employment brand.

Mika sees it a little differently. She says at this point there are so many people trying to get jobs and so many people on the inside who might be getting the job that it's not so much about HR people and interviewers lacking civility as it is the fact that there's no time to deal with what she calls "the incoming." And we, the unemployed, are the incoming. According to Mika,

It's rough to deal with, and it's really hard to understand that when you're looking for a job, because of course your entire day is consumed waiting for that phone call that may never happen. It takes mental gymnastics every day to stay up, and most of the times during the job hunt there is no reason to be up, so it's very difficult not to be prone to depression in the process. So, I think the lack of civility that you can point to is not because people are more mean-spirited than they ever were. Let's face it, business is tough when you're trying to make deals, hire people, fire people, make things happen. Business has always been tough—look at the show *Mad Men*—and it used to be a lot tougher for women. I think it's just now the amount of people in your position versus the amount of jobs that fit the bill and fit your skills is out of balance.

Mentoring—Is It Right for You?

Finding a mentor or mentoring someone during this difficult time can help bring the goodness of humanity back into perspective and make things more civil. My friend Adam Krumwiede picked up a mentor without even looking for one while interviewing for a high-level media planning job. Actually, his new mentor chose him. It was a humbling experience, and the relationship took root during a job interview that was unfortunately going south at the time.

The position was for a senior advertising media buyer, the person responsible for purchasing media space or time, as well as developing the campaign and researching how it will be most effective for the marketer. The company was looking for someone quite special who could hold the title of executive vice president for the third-largest media-buying company in the country. He met with the head of HR and took the obligatory questions in good stride. He remembers it being uncomfortably warm in the room that day. The thermostat read eighty degrees. He remembers worrying about how he would hold up for the next two interviews that were sure to be progressively more challenging. He was starting to sweat.

He made it to his third and final interview for the day with the company's COO. The interview started off well, but near the end the interviewer stopped and said, "Listen, I'm going to be straightforward, and give you some immediate feedback."

Krumwiede says, " . . . and then came this queasy, sinking feeling in my stomach; I knew I wasn't getting the job today!" Krumwiede sheepishly smiles as he says this.

When he stopped, I knew he wasn't going to say, "Congratulations, boy I love you, how much money do you want?" It's more like, where did I screw up here—was I rambling too much, was it the heat, sweat was coming down my face. I must have looked like crap.

He did something I wasn't expecting, though. He leaned in and said to me, "You've got a great résumé here on paper, but you're not telling your story well in person."

I nearly fell out of my chair. All this immediate disappointment was crushing down on me when I realized I wasn't walking out of here with a job but here was this very respectable executive reaching out to help me do better.

What I realized is that this kind of feedback is gold dust, something very few people offer. He said to me, "Hey I like you and I want to help you." The next morning I drafted a thank-you note and shot it to him, and he responded right back and said I'm glad you sent this because I was about ready to pick up the phone to call you today. So I said to him let me spend some time thinking about my story, and I'll take you up on your offer to help me make it better.

The takeaway here is that this executive is offering to help him on his own dime and in the spirit of mentorship and paying it forward, and that is impressive. Looking back, Krumwiede thinks what his new mentor was saying was he wasn't the right person at this time for this role. "He never said never for future opportunities."

Recognize the Gold Nuggets

The meat and potatoes for me is you never know what valuable nuggets you will uncover during an interview. You may not walk away with a job, but maybe you walk away with something even more important, without even knowing it or understanding it at the time. One of the best interviewing experiences I have had—and sorry to say ultimately did not lead to a job—was with eCommerce/WalmartLabs.

Far and away the best talent sourcing person I ever had the pleasure speaking with was a man named Stephen Shearman from Walmart. A former colleague referred me to Shearman for an internal communications position based in the heart of Silicon Valley at Walmart's high-tech labs. The world's largest retailer, with 2.2 million associates and ten thousand stores around the globe, has been boosting its e-commerce capabilities with an eye to one day surpassing the mother of all e-commerce retailers, Amazon. Walmart admits it might take twenty-five years to get there, but then again you don't turn around a $470 billion retailer overnight. As it stands now, the company expects to generate $9 billion in global e-commerce revenue in its next fiscal year, ending January 31, 2014. Amazon's revenues topped $61 billion for 2012.

Walmart's innovation labs are made up of a tight group of engineering teams whose only mission is to develop from the ground up technology that will make Walmart an Internet destination of choice among e-shoppers. They have even designed their own search engine to make it easier for customers to use their smartphones to find deals and comparison shop.

The position I was interviewing for supported the CEO of Walmart Global eCommerce group as well as developed communications strategy for the Walmart eCommerce organization both in the United States and in several key international markets such as China and Brazil. What caught my eye was the fact that whoever got tapped for this position would have the opportunity to build a true e-commerce community for the functions in each of Walmart's markets. I was qualified for the job in the broad sense of the word, but I was up against people who once again specialized exclusively in running internal communications departments within large companies. Some of these candidates had ten to fifteen years' experience specifically running internal communications.

Shearman took about ten minutes to explain very clearly the ground rules of our interview and went into great detail about the benefits of working for Walmart. His presentation was flawless and delivered in a comforting accent that was influenced by the Deep South.

"Hello Dwain, good afternoon, Stephen Shearman calling from Walmart, how are you sir? So, do I have the right day and the right time? I'm calling from Arkansas."

"Gosh, I thought you were on the West Coast, so in the e-mail I put in Pacific Time. Sorry about that . . . "

"Dwain, I'm looking forward to hearing more about your background and talk to you about the position and answer any questions I can, but if we could first, if I could, maybe we could go over a few HR questions like relocation, compensation, timing, and if we're not *aligned* on some of these issues, we will know it right up front. How does that sound to you?

"I want you to know that I don't assume anything other than we are going to talk about the communications position, and we'll see if there might be an interest on both sides to take this to the next level . . . "

Wow. It was the most refreshing hourlong conversation I had ever had with an HR professional. He was up-front and transparent about the interview process and explained in satisfactory detail what the expectations were for the job. He was also honest about

Walmart's hesitancy to hire somebody outside of the Silicon Valley "bubble."

I made my case as simple to understand as possible. I posed the question, "Why would Walmart want to hire somebody who has been doing the same thing for ten or fifteen years, in this case managing an internal communications department, who has become stale, churning over old ideas, when they could hire someone like me who brings a fresh perspective and broader skill set to the position?"

Regarding the Silicon bubble, I reiterated my hypothesis, "Why hire the same old, same old thinking that lives in that isolating ecosystem? Bring in somebody with a different worldview who will innovate and shake things up."

I could tell he liked what he was hearing, and he wrapped up the call by saying that he would take the information from our conversation and present me to the hiring manager. He felt that I was a qualified candidate and would get back to me within the week as to next steps. I thanked him for his time and complimented him on his professionalism.

True to his word, Shearman responded within the week. Unfortunately, the news was not to my liking. But I will give Walmart this: it was a class-act rejection letter. Here it is:

Dwain,

Thank you for your interest in this position with Walmart.

The hiring team has considered and reviewed your résumé and unfortunately there were other candidates, whose credentials and experiences better align to this position's unique requirements, making them more qualified for this position. You do possess valuable skills and experiences that could be ideal for future opportunities. I would like to retain your résumé and cross reference your skills and experiences for other opportunities as they arise.

We understand the news of not being selected can be disappointing. We hope you will consider Walmart as a career option in the future. I would like to encourage you to go to the Walmart Corporate Career site, (http://careers.walmart.com/our-corporate-opportunities/) create a profile with your résumé and utilize the "search alert" feature that will alert you via email when a position matching your search criteria is available and posted on the career site. By creating a profile, you are searchable to the 100+ Walmart recruiters when they search for qualified candidates for their open position. If you do find a position and apply, [here's the classy part—seriously] please advise me via email so I can monitor your application process, liaise with the recruiter and hiring team and provide you status updates as they become available.

Thank you for your time and interest.

I haven't spoken to Shearman since I received his e-mail. We are connected on LinkedIn, and I know if I ever come across a job of interest at Walmart or get an urge to move to Arkansas he is my go-to guy.

Take a Stand

Sometimes you have to put your foot down during an interview and take a stand for what you believe in or how you think you should be treated and then let the chips fall where they may. A very talented friend of mine, Mike Mezquida, who used to be my cameraman when I was a local TV news reporter in Connecticut, shares an experience that makes me chuckle every time I think about it.

Mezquida put down the camera years ago to become a video editor for ABC network news in Washington, DC. He also worked for many years as a local newspaper writer, so when he saw an opportunity on craigslist to work for an Internet news company, he jumped at the chance. He knew he could do the job, so he submitted some sample articles to the online editor in chief. He had been underemployed for more than a year and was desperate to nail down a full-time job. The pay was dreadful, but the job was interesting, and perhaps it could lead to other things.

He landed a meeting. While waiting in the lobby for the interview, he overheard the editor says over the phone, "I can't talk right now. I'm testing someone this morning."

Mezquida says to me, "'Test, REALLY?' and right then and there," he says, "I started getting angry. You have to understand, I have more than twenty years' experience reporting the news, and by now I had been turned down for so many jobs that at this point my hopes weren't very high getting this either."

Mezquida decides to do something I couldn't imagine doing myself—not that I haven't fantasized doing it on several occasions. In fairness and to set this up correctly, Mezquida had provided the editor with a thorough portfolio of writing samples and references. He was unquestionably a pro.

> I was so convinced that I wasn't going to get that job, and I was so angry at having to take a test for a $28,000 per year job that I just got fed up and told the editor off and that testing me was demeaning. They wanted me to watch a video of a city council meeting and write about it, take a spelling and grammar test, go out and cover three stories

and report back. I flat out made up my mind I wasn't going to have any part of that. And, because I was convinced at that point I wasn't going to get the job anyway, this could be my first interview where I finally let an employer get a taste of their own medicine. I will turn them down first. I will give them a piece of my mind on the way out the door and I got up and grabbed my stuff and started to leave without saying goodbye!

A funny thing happened though. The editor liked what she was hearing and asked that he stay.

"I think she liked that I stood up for myself. They pulled together an offer. Now, I didn't get the job, because I ended up taking another one, but in this case the confidence that I showed, bordering on arrogance, actually worked in my favor."

My friend took a chance—partly because he stood up for what he believed in and partly because he was fed up with how employers have treated him. I suspect most interviewers' jaws would've dropped to the floor, and they would have been rendered speechless. Maybe Mezquida's moxie persuaded this employer that he's good, and only somebody who is that good could be so self-confident to pull off that performance.

It doesn't hurt to mix it up once in a while. If you've been on enough interviews, you know you've tried it all. You've smiled a lot, not smiled too much. You've been talkative and not so talkative. If you're a woman, you've worn your hair up, you've worn it down and to the side. Every interview is different, and every hiring manager is different. After a while we try different things to relate to the person we're interviewing with. I'm not suggesting the next interview you go on, be sure to tell the interviewer to take this job and shove it. Be yourself. Experiment. Try to relax and enjoy the process or, as reinvention coach Pamela Mitchell suggests, be present for the journey.

What You Might Try Asking the Hiring Manager After an Interview

Try asking the hiring manager one of these questions before exiting the interview. You will come away with valuable information and more often than not impress the interviewer with having the skill to address any objections he might have right up front. Nine times out of ten the interviewer won't even think to share this information unless prodded to do so. If you learn you have fallen short in a few areas as a result of asking the question(s), you are now armed to clarify your qualifications or clear up inconsistencies or misunderstandings, which will hopefully give you the edge.

- ✓ Do you see any gaps in my qualifications that I need to fill?
- ✓ Are there any reasons I'm not fully qualified for this position?
- ✓ Is there anything I've said today that might hurt my chances of being hired here?
- ✓ Now that you've had a chance to meet and interview me, what reservations would you have in putting me in this position?
- ✓ What have I said during today's interview that's inconsistent with your perfect candidate for this job?

7

LOSE TO WIN

Weight, That Is

Nearly every morning at 7:30 sharp, I drive my two daughters to middle school. It's a scenic three-mile ramble down a windy wooded road that hugs Westport's Saugatuck River. In the summer fly fishermen wade thigh-deep into the slow-moving water, casting for brook and brown trout. It's an idyllic setting and the perfect out-of-the-way location for the headquarters of the world's largest hedge fund. Nestled on the banks of the river sits the campus of Bridgewater Associates. Bridgewater manages assets totaling more than $130 billion. Every morning I drive past the company, I look over and think about what it would be like to work there. The thought of somehow being connected to that much money sends chills down my spine— all the more so because a real paycheck hasn't hit my account in nearly a year.

When I lost my job, I scoured their career site in hopes of finding anything related to marketing or public relations. Nothing jumped out, but then again a company like Bridgewater doesn't exactly fit my profile. I'm never going to be mistaken for a finance guy, even though I live in a town overflowing with number crunchers. I had to take Algebra twice to take Algebra 2 once and survived the experience by the skin of my teeth. I was never good at handling money either—investing money, counting money, and now, as you can see, making money. Math was always a mystery to me. Even the simplest subtraction problems can trip me up. My kids are great at math and love to tease me into helping them with their homework. "Dad, I need you to walk me through solving this one: $ax^2 + bx + c = 0$," my son says.

Very funny, but I don't feel completely out of place as a right-brain person who graduated with a liberal arts degree. Westport is also home to plenty of creative people. Many entertainers, authors, and celebrities choose Westport for its close proximity to New York and its beautiful shoreline. The likes of Paul Newman, Joanne Woodward, Michael Douglas, F. Scott Fitzgerald, Martha Stewart, Robert Redford, and master of the thriller, novelist Robert Ludlum, have all lived and thrived in Westport over the years.

So, Bridgewater is probably not for me.

I'm not a numbers guy, but I am an apple pie guy, and it's showing everywhere. It's also killing me on the interview circuit. I'm squirming and bulging in the only suit that semi-fits. Even with the trouser button open, it's hardly bearable. At least my belt buckle hides the evidence, sort of. I feel like my backside is going to bust out at any moment, like bending over the interviewer's desk while handing over my résumé. When I was let go from my job, I was at the heaviest I had ever been in my life—too heavy to even want to say here. I had taken on the sedentary corporate lifestyle that many people in highly developed countries do, forgoing almost all physical activity. Of course, this had nothing to do with living in a developed country. I wasn't getting to the gym or eating healthy food. I'm not a lazy person, but over the years I had let myself become a "fat fuck," as Susie Essman's character Susie Greene likes to call her husband Jeff, Larry David's manager, on *Curb Your Enthusiasm*.

Like a lot of people who work in front of the computer in an office and drive their car back and forth to work each day, it's important to take the time to exercise at least four days a week. In a 2012 study presented by Qibin Qi at the American Heart Association's Epidemiology and Prevention/Nutrition, Physical Activity and Metabolism 2012 conference in San Diego scientific sessions, Qi reported that a sedentary lifestyle amplifies a genetic disposition to obesity. The good news is, he said, that walking briskly and briefly each day can cut that effect in half. Somebody isn't getting the message, considering that the Centers for Disease Control keep saying that a third of American adults are overweight and another third are obese, totaling a combined 68.8 percent. Obesity is also a contributing factor in five out of the ten top causes of death: heart disease, cancer, stroke, diabetes, and kidney disease. What's even more disturbing, according to the CDC, is that one in three children born in our country in the year 2000 will develop diabetes sometime in their lives.

In Mika's new book *Obsessed: America's Food Addiction—and My Own*, coauthored by Diane Smith, she writes about how fat children often grow into fat adults. She explains that this is becoming a national security challenge for our country, and Mission: Readiness, an organization of retired senior military officers, is committing investments to combat the problem. The organization calculates that nine million young people ages seventeen to twenty-seven are "too fat to fight." This means one-quarter of that age group is too heavy to be accepted into the military. It has been said more than once that obesity may be our nation's greatest national security threat, and folks at the White House are taking notice.

Mika also reports that annual medical expenditures attributable to obesity run as high as $147 billion per year, according to researchers at RTI International, the Agency for Healthcare Research and Quality, and the CDC.

Losing the Weight to Regain My Edge

The statistics are sobering and overwhelming. We are becoming a zombie land of lard asses. My words, not hers. And damned if you wouldn't know, I've become one of them. But I still have good excuses as to why I packed on the pounds. In addition to my hard-earned sedentary lifestyle, I had developed what started out as an arthritic right knee and turned into a full-blown collapsed joint, bone-on-bone throbbing leg from hell. The uncontrollable pain was excruciating only when I stood, sat, walked, or breathed. I stupidly put up with this condition for more than a year. The doctors leave it up to you to decide when to pull the trigger on the surgery. They are happy to advise you along the way once the condition is diagnosed, and they know what to do once you say operate, but they're smart enough to stay away altogether from giving the tiniest hint of what you're in for when it comes to the postoperative pain.

In three words, *death is sweeter*. It took more than four weeks for the ache to subside enough to feel like a human being again and then another six months of physical therapy to work out the stiffness and straighten out the knee completely. You don't stop eating during this, by the way. I had gone on two weeks' short-term disability to cover the surgery and went back to work sooner than I should have. Six months after getting my new knee, I was let go.

I remember looking in the mirror and feeling like this horrible Humpty Dumpty–like person was looking back at me. I'm exaggerating, but just a little. At close to 6' 4" I can do a pretty good job of hiding the excess fat. But that was for the outside world. For me, I couldn't stand looking at myself anymore. What was worse, I had lined up an interview with a world-renowned brand to do major consumer-facing PR work. I was mortified. Not because I lacked confidence in my ability to do the job, but I felt I wasn't putting my best foot forward with how I looked. My weight was chipping away at my self-esteem. I didn't look good; therefore, I didn't feel good. And, when you don't feel good, that comes across in every aspect of your life. My face was puffy from the salty snacks and sweets I had been eating during my convalescence. You can dress for success all you want, but if your dress is looking more like a muumuu than a business suit, you're sending the wrong message in the interview.

"When you walk into a room looking good, you're sending the message about yourself that says, 'I have my act together,'" Mika says, who reveals her own lifelong struggle with food, dieting, and body image in her book. "Whether employed or unemployed, when you walk through that door for the first time to meet your potential boss and you're overweight, study after study shows that you're being discriminated against, and people feel that there is something wrong with you, that you are undisciplined and that your life is a mess."

I walked through that door at that major brand feeling the way Mika describes. I remember sitting in the interview thinking how I couldn't wait to unfasten my top shirt button so I could breathe. My skills and experience brought me back to the interview table three times, but in the end I didn't get the job. I don't think it was because I looked like a stand-in for Susie Greene's husband in *Curb*, but, as I hoofed it back to Grand Central Terminal in New York, I swore I would be at least ten pounds lighter come my next face-to-face interview. That was the goal, anyway. And, speaking of stand-ins, at my heaviest there were more than three occasions that people would stop me on the street and say I looked like Tony Soprano from the HBO hit series *The Sopranos*. They would ask me if I was the late actor James Gandolfini. Come on?

I was angry at myself. I was angry because my weight was now punishing me professionally and possibly limiting my options for landing the job of my dreams. Now, along with the stress that comes with unemployment, I needed to double down and lose weight. A lot of weight and quickly.

Mika never saw me prior to losing the weight, but when we spoke on the phone she laughed at the irony of trying to lose weight while unemployed, when in essence you're spending a lot of time sitting around on the computer, in the car driving to interviews, or in my case at the beach hiding out hoping no one will see me. Mika said:

> Being fit when you're unemployed is so difficult because you have all the time in the world to walk through the kitchen and, as you know, people eat when they're depressed. The fact that you lost so much weight shows me that you have what it takes to make it, and you will make it. Because if you can

be fit under these circumstances, you should be back in the workforce. Every tiny bit of messaging counts, and you've got to give it your best. You can't go into an interview looking your worst physically. I tell people they have to work as hard on getting fit and watching their weight as they do looking for a job.

My goal was to lose forty pounds as quickly and as healthily as possible. I confess I was looking for a get-skinny-quick diet to jump-start my new commitment to lose that weight. I figured dropping 10 percent of my excess body weight in short order would motivate me to change my eating habits and get me well on my way to where I wanted to be. I had heard on the radio about a diet plan that sounded too good to be true. It was being touted by a local morning talk radio host who was known for his love of food but wanted to lose weight for his son's upcoming wedding. On my drive into work every weekday morning during his morning news show, he talked about the progress he was making with this terrific woman named Irina Gosh, a certified practitioner of the Sadkhin Complex. I was surprised to learn that her office was conveniently based in Westport. The radio host was also videotaping his appointments and showing them on the radio station's website to rally listeners in support of his effort. It was paying off. He lost twenty pounds in ten days.

I finally built up the courage to call for an appointment. I was nervous, reserved on the phone. I had never enrolled in a diet program before. A woman with an eastern European accent answered my cell. It was Gosh.

The plan was for me to come in for a brief consultation that included watching a short video to decide whether I wanted to start the program. I set up a time to come in. "America, you have to have balls to lose weight!" the announcer on the video said. You heard that right. That's the secret behind the Sadkhin diet—tiny steel balls. The diet practitioner tapes a tiny ball to a predetermined pressure point behind the ear. When rubbed, the pressure point encourages the hypothalamus gland to release hormones that cause you to feel full, or so says Gosh. The diet consists of acupressure therapy and taking in the correct amount of protein, fruits, and vegetables. "You alternate two days of fruits and vegetables and two days of whole milk, while making sure to rotate the tiny spheres every two hours blocking the hunger," Gosh says in her Ukrainian accent. Even though I saw the success the news talk show host was having with the program, I'm skeptical. "So what are the skeptics talking about, that you're going to lose weight too fast?" Gosh says to me with a mischievous smile. "The diet is all natural, 100 percent noninvasive, and acupressure has been around for centuries with zero side effects. You're eating fruits and vegetables for your source of vitamins and minerals, and you're getting your protein from milk."

The diet immediately starts working for me. When I stick to the strict rotation schedule, I notice my appetite immediately drops to a dull roar. So far I'm surviving on less than two pounds of fruit and vegetables a day and, on my protein days, I'm surviving on three or four glasses of milk, max. The inches melted away, and at my first weigh-in I was ten pounds lighter than when I started the regimen. I couldn't believe how easy it was. I was well on my way to my goal weight. I had more energy, and I felt good because I was taking care of myself. My suits were fitting better. I felt more confident. Within a couple of months I had dropped thirty-eight pounds.

For me, healthy eating has always been a struggle, because it's easy to default to junk food and make bad decisions when I'm on the fly. I constantly tell myself to keep that in mind three times a day. The benefit of the diet is, once I broke myself of the habit of eating sugar and processed food, I stop craving it. There is no magic to keeping the weight off on this diet, either. I'm in charge of cooking what I eat (or my wife is, I should say, lucky for me), and the key is to combine foods properly and to make healthy choices. There's this to think about too: "The reason most of my clients never gain the weight back is because they will never, ever go back to their bad habits after struggling with their weight for many, many years and finally they are happy about the way they feel and see how easy it is to lose it with this program," Gosh says.

It works for me. That doesn't mean it's right for everyone. I have transitioned my eating habits more to what is sometimes referred to as a paleo or primal diet. I learned about the diet through some friends who are on the same nonprofit organization board I am on. Several years ago I had great success following the advice of health and fitness expert Mark Sisson, publisher of the acclaimed book *The Primal Blueprint* and MarksDailyApple.com, a popular health blog that garners millions of page views each month. His book started it all for me. Sisson has made a real name for himself in challenging many flawed elements of what he calls the "normal conventional wisdom" about diet and exercise.

Unless you have spent a little time educating yourself about the paleo diet concept, I expect you're about to have your nutritional belief system seriously turned on its head. But if you stay with me and are open to the idea that much of what you learned about nutrition could be wrong—not all wrong, but skewed—you might get excited about something that could change your life and give you more energy than you ever imagined, as it did for me.

Sisson's *primal* theme encourages people to reconnect with their hunter-gatherer ancestral roots. We're talking cavemen: eating natural plant and animal foods, getting plenty of low-level daily activity interspersed with occasional brief, intense exercise, and engaging in lifestyle behaviors that balance the stress of hectic modern life. Sisson says two million years of evolution have led us to where we now each possess the genes to build a perfect, healthy, happy human form. When I spoke to him at his home in Malibu, California, he told me that for the last ten thousand years our ancestors lived on unprocessed food; only in the last hundred years did we start eating industrialized food and living more sedentary lives, adversely affecting our health, productivity, and libido. His primal blueprint pulls together the tenets of informed biological evolution, traditional wisdom, and science to help people eat and sleep in a modern world in a healthy, sustainable, and enjoyable way.

Sisson's primal research and teachings were the invention that met the mother of all necessity. Although he was an elite marathoner (2:18) and triathlete (fourth at Hawaii Ironman), he was constantly sick and injured, had osteoarthritis in his feet and tendonitis in his hips, and suffered irritable bowel syndrome and seasonal allergies.

Today he's become a new man by practicing what he preaches, and he's not a preachy guy. His teaching style is based on the law of attraction, not conversion. He's simply putting the information out there. Sisson is about maximizing every aspect of your health.

"You can't go out into this world and perform well at a job, be a good husband or wife, be a good parent, a good mate, if you are in poor health, if you don't have the energy and the mental acuity or faculties necessary to perform at your maximum strength. It's so critical that you recognize that taking care of yourself and eating right is your number one job." There's nothing selfish about this, he says, because

> it's about recognizing you can't perform any of your other tasks unless or until you are healthy.
>
> You can try. You can get away with it for a while if you're unhealthy, but at some point it will bite you in the rear end. Guys and gals who are out of work—and I tell those people all the time that if you have lost your job, it is important to get your act together and focus for the next six weeks on your health and regaining your health—returning yourself to what you define peak performance is for you.

With the primal diet, the more meat, seafood, and vegetable options you provide for yourself, the better. Don't forget the fruit either. This is no Atkins diet, but it does have some similarities when it comes to bulking up on more proteins than carbs. But, be sure to leave out grains in any form. Sisson points out that grains were not part of the human diet prior to the agricultural revolution. Humans didn't evolve eating grains, which is to say our digestive processes didn't evolve to maximize the effectiveness of grain consumption. What's more, people don't realize the havoc grains play with insulin and other hormones in our bodies. His grain theory surprises me, so I ask him why it is we are being led to believe through advertising campaigns and government food pyramids that grains are good for us.

"People have their habits and belief systems," he says.

If you're a person who loves your steel cut oatmeal in the morning, it's going to take a lot of convincing to get you to change your mind, especially if your doctor says the paleo way to live is a lot of hokum and you don't need to follow it. People in general aren't good at interpreting science. I feel it's my job to take this information and the science and make it palatable so everybody can understand it or at least read the book. It's not easy for most of us to think counterintuitively. Most of the world still lives on grain, but that doesn't mean it's good for you.

The lifestyle is simple to stick to—just follow the rules of living ten thousand years ago. Here is Sisson's original ten Primal Blueprint Laws:

1. Eat lots of animals, plants (and insects)—This covers protein, fats, carbs, vitamins, minerals, antioxidants, fiber, water, and other nutrients necessary to sustain life. This diet provided all the necessary fuel, and our ancestors developed strong muscles through a life of hunting, gathering, and fight-or-flight experience to keep them on their toes.

2. Move around a lot at a slow pace—Our ancestors stayed healthy by moving about, hunting several hours a day at a low level aerobic pace. Sisson says this low level of activity built stronger muscle cells, enabling people to store excess food as fat but also to readily convert the stored fat back into energy. Sisson gets a dig in, telling me our cavemen brothers and sisters didn't go out and jog at 80 percent of their max heart rate for long periods of time, as conventional wisdom suggests today!

3. Lift heavy things—Theirs was a lifestyle of foraging, carrying firewood, toting heavy spears, and dragging heavy carcasses back to the campfire. Women also got in on the act. Who do you think carried the babies all day?

4. Run really fast every once in a while—Avoiding charging saber-toothed tigers and other beasts made for a world of danger that tested our ancestors' ability to run fast for short distances. This built up the necessary strength to live a long caveman life or die trying.

5. Get lots of sleep—Sisson says our ancestors also enjoyed plenty of sleep, and it is likely they slept together as families or as small tribes, keeping watch for predators throughout the night. He claims long days of hunting and otherwise working hard for food also required sufficient time to recover.

6. Play—Our ancestors worked hard, and they played hard in the form of social interaction that included wrestling and spear and rock throwing for sport. Women would spend time grooming each other, which provided the net effect of solidifying social bonds that helped prompt the release of endorphins to diffuse the stress of the life-threatening situations they lived with every day.

7. Get some sunlight every day—Most of their time was spent outdoors, so cavemen were regularly exposed to the sun and vitamin D, which the body needs and can't obtain from food.

8. Avoid trauma—Trauma or lapse in judgment, Sisson says, was probably most responsible for the low average life expectancy of our ancestors, despite their otherwise good health. Being aware of whatever immediate action needed to be taken, whether it was running from a predator or avoiding falling rocks, a broken ankle could be the demise of a caveman who can no longer run from danger.

9. Avoid poisonous things—New foods, snakes, and insects all posed a danger, but Sisson says luckily our ancestors' keen sense of smell and taste also helped sort out a lot of potential problems.

10. Use your mind—Our intellectual ability attributable to an increase in brain size over the generations helped our ancestors become more resilient and work out more complex problems. They developed language, tools, and better hunting methods over thousands of years that helped them live longer, more productive lives.

A friend of mine took up the primal lifestyle shortly after I started writing this book. His weight had him so down in the dumps that he didn't even bother looking for interviews after he was laid off. He spent ten months doing nothing on the job front! He was ashamed of how he looked. I wouldn't call him morbidly obese, but he was definitely too heavy, heavier than I was when I started my weight loss journey. I could see by looking at him how someone would instantly pass judgment that this person had "control" issues. It wasn't fair because he is a great guy, a very talented guy who deserves to be working just like me.

He talked to me about his self-hatred for weighing three hundred–plus pounds and how it was affecting every aspect of his life. "I didn't want to put myself in front of people because of the shame associated with this part of me. I just can't see people right now in my current shape."

He shared with me his bouts with suicidal thoughts relating to being "fat" and jobless:

> I ask myself sometimes whether life is really worth living. I have periods when I think about my indifference to living. I definitely have my depressing moments. In my case I don't think I would act on it. The other challenge is I don't know how to even go about looking for a job. It's totally foreign to me. I've never had to do it, so I feel isolated and to some extent I think I'm using my weight as an excuse not to look for work. Who wants to hire somebody who's been out of work for a year—and is fat!

"Don't answer that!" he says with a growling smile on his face.

● **FORTUNATELY FOR MY FRIEND** he has started to get back in shape. He is eating healthier and following the primal way of eating as close as he can. He let me know he's left the insects off the meal plan at home. I see him at a coffee shop and immediately notice the difference the diet is having on his waistline. "If it comes in a bag I don't eat it," he says to me as he hugs his diminishing belly. "I stopped eating sugar, white flour, rice, anything white—mostly cut out all carbs except for fruit." He says the other secret to his success is making time to exercise again. It's not going to happen overnight, but he's on the right track, and that seems to be putting him in a better mind-set. He's starting to network more and go on interviews. The last I spoke with him, he was going back for seconds with Morgan Stanley and Deutsche Bank—second interviews that is.

Move It to Make It: Exercise Is Key

He's right about exercise. I try to ride my bike three days a week at the very least. I must confess that I still hate being seen at the gym by the neighborhood, especially in the middle of the day when I should be at work! I still can't help wondering what they must think to themselves. I bring this up to my wife and she laughs, "Do you think they are spending one second wondering about what you're doing?" Wow, thanks for the reality check. "They've got their own world and problems to deal with." Maybe she's right. I'm not the center of the universe like I think sometimes.

I switched to the bike after having my knee replaced. Mika says that's not enough. I temper what she says, coming from someone who runs four miles a day and runs full and half marathons in between hosting *Morning Joe*, giving speeches, making personal appearances around the globe, spearheading woman's initiatives and conferences, and writing best-selling books (three and counting).

Her motto is, move, move often, take the stairs, walk, walk, walk wherever you go. "Nearly every weight loss plan includes exercise, and experts tell me that you need to be pedaling that bike to town and back three hours a week. So, get on the stick," she says.

Ask any successful businessperson what keeps her sharp, and I bet you part of the answer will include some kind of daily workout regime.

I put the question to Joe Echevarria, CEO of Deloitte LLP. Echevarria is the epitome of success. And he works out whenever he gets the chance. He's the first to say every day for him was hard economic times growing up as a latchkey kid of Puerto Rican descent in the South Bronx, just eight miles from where he sits today in his corner office at 30 Rockefeller Center in Midtown. He joined the Deloitte US firms as an accountant in 1978 and became an audit partner in 1988. In 2011, he was named chief executive officer of Deloitte LLP.

> "For me my career has been nothing more than a journey of passion. *Passion* and *paranoia*," he says with a slight grin. "At any moment this could all change, and I could go back to that kid who, in just one wrong turn, could have wound up like everybody else. There were essentially only three kids who wound up making it out of my neighborhood. One was a basketball player, one became a male model and photographer, and one owns a restaurant chain."

Echevarria applies the same kind of discipline to his exercise routine that he applies to his work. He runs and works out hard with weights. "I told my wife I want to live to be 110 years old." Why 110? "That's my goal so if I work towards that maybe I can get to 85." Now that's some kind of accounting loophole, say I.

Exercise is a given for real estate developer and media mogul Mortimer B. Zuckerman. Not a day goes by that he isn't taking time out to stretch and ride his bike. His diet also plays a huge role in keeping him focused and fit. "I'm happy to say I became a vegan three and a half years ago, and I lost thirty pounds in the process—not that I was that heavy, but I weigh now what I weighed when I got out of college. I feel unbelievably energized. It's just fantastic!"

Zuckerman tells me on the phone that the only thing job seekers can do is double their search efforts and never give up trying to get ahead. He also brings the conversation back to the importance of eating right and staying fit to overcome the hardships. "It gets very difficult after a while, but you have to keep yourself in some kind of physical shape. You will feel good if you get back into physical shape; you'll have more energy to go out and look for a job. Shoe leather is very, very important here, so you just can't give up on this. You cannot give up!"

8

LIFE GOES ON

The Social Life of the Unemployed

Facing Rock Bottom

Money was not the problem as I sat in front of my computer searching for a job one week before Thanksgiving. I was irritable, restless, and my mood had gotten progressively worse leading up to the holiday. It didn't help that the thermometer on my desk read sixty-three degrees, cold as a meat locker in my basement office.

That night I was feeling especially sorry for myself and somehow had worked out in my mind that I would fly to my parent's house to spend this Thanksgiving away from them all, as if it were punishment for something they had perpetrated against me. The holiday season was bringing out the worst in me. I felt disconnected from my three kids and most of my friends. In fact, in recent months I had managed to shun relationships including my wife, who by now felt like the time was *right* to call in a hostage negotiator or make a break for it.

I had read enough self-help books over the years that suggest you don't get any happier by making lots of money. You get happier because you *accomplish* something that makes you feel worthwhile, and the result of accomplishing something makes you money. Translation: money rules the world, but you will go stark raving mad if you don't achieve something or further yourself as a human being and provide something to someone, anything— provide for the sake of providing if you have to, but do *something*. What was I accomplishing being out of work? Nothing! I was pissed. Unemployment, once and for all, proved to me that I was and forever will be a workaholic who draws all self-worth from his work. As shortsighted as that is, I'm far from being alone on that one.

I kept telling my wife that I can't find peace in my head. "What does that mean?" she would always ask. "You're upset because you don't have a job—it's not about peace." I would walk away and say to myself, this woman has no fucking idea how depressed I'm getting. Nothing was working for me. Worse yet, *I* still wasn't working. I felt like shit. That was the whole point. My life was the epitome of abeyance. I had gone from feeling moderately miserable over the past few months to feeling objectionably horrible. Enough was enough. Being out of work was killing me and taking its toll in ways I hadn't imagined possible.

Utter despair was what I woke up to everyday. I felt trapped in my head. I found myself pacing the house, looking out onto the street from our living room bay window with a feeling that I was trapped inside a jail cell. I could go out but I didn't want to anymore. I was isolating, and the more miserable I made myself feel, the more I found myself wanting to isolate. It was a vicious circle. Was I going mad? NO. I was out of work . . . for too long now. We were blowing through our savings—our cash was gone, and we were now liquidating what stocks and mutual funds we had saved over the years, leaving the 401(k) as a last resort—the penalties to cash out were offensive to me, *as if that sensibility mattered as we sat there figuring out how to keep the lights on.*

By now I had dismissed the significance of our diminishing nest egg. It's not that money no longer mattered—it did. It's just that I had become numb over the fact that I no longer had a traditional "job" that paid a traditional income and that the world I was now living in, the job search world, had become so flat that there was nothing on the horizon as far as my eyes could see. I was losing all hope that I would find another job in my field. How was I to pay the bills, especially with one kid several years away from applying to colleges? The new currency I traded in was job rejection e-mails. I was mostly overqualified for what jobs I could find on Internet job boards.

Another dirty secret of this recession is that a guy like me is often considered a flight risk to employers who have openings. Whether real or perceived, they are afraid to hire someone with my experience for fear that I will leave when the economy picks up—presumably for a better-paying job. Everywhere I look there are companies I could work for who have positions open.

The reality is the company is losing out on the enormous talents of highly skilled people sitting on the sidelines who are happy to have a job after being out of work for a year or more. Educated white-collar workers who are dying to get back into the workforce, like me, who can provide employers what they want for less in this *new* economy.

I keep at it though. My fingers started to go numb at my keyboard from the chill of the basement. The space heater was breaking down like everything else in my world. Sitting there freezing at my desk suddenly made me think in metaphors: how in my current state I've become the man who can no longer be the provider of fire. Like the bone-crushing Yukon cold in many of Jack London's stories, unemployment had become the ultimate antagonist in the current narrative of my life, a foe against which I had been pitted for survival. Unemployment does not act deliberately. Like nature, it simply is, but, as a result of world events, politics, and the economy—one could even say my own folly—it was as if tonight I was facing my own death sentence. I thought at that moment I truly didn't want to live anymore. I was melting into the upstairs foyer wallpaper and in my mind had become a useless nonparticipant, nonmember of the family. *I was better off dead*, I thought. No one would even notice. I had *thoroughly* convinced myself of that.

And then it happened.

My cell phone rang. On the other end was a close friend from California who said he needed to be convinced not to shoot himself. He said he was going to put his gun in his mouth when he hung up.

This was no joke. He was in crisis. He never talked like this. I know him for his sarcastic sense of humor, love of sports, and conservative political opinions. I knew he was not going through a happy time in his life, but he was the last person I would suspect to be feeling suicidal. His call almost instantly snapped me out of my own funk, as I frantically searched for my own bearings so I could learn why he had suddenly lost his.

Without even asking I knew what had set him off. He was one of us—or at least he was *one of me.* I never thought about it, but he was in a situation similar to my own. He wasn't completely unemployed but rather he belonged to what is commonly referred to as the underemployed class. He worked on and off as a freelance copywriter for ad agencies—a business he had been in forever and a job he was great at. The work he was finding these days was beneath him, but it was all he could get since being laid off as a highly paid creative director.

He did something stupid. He turned fifty.

I knew he had been living paycheck to paycheck for quite a while, and, when he wasn't chasing down job opportunities or actually doing the work he had landed, he was e-mailing his résumé to potential employers and networking to get on with an agency that offered benefits and steady work. He is a talented, seasoned, and experienced creative. But in this job market that didn't mean much. He was struggling to scrape together enough money to pay monthly bills on time—or at all.

I had heard two months ago that he had been interviewing in Los Angeles for a highly respected midsized ad agency. He had gone through two successful rounds of interviews. He had met with four senior people during this first set of interviews and returned for a second day to meet with one of the agency's creative directors.

He was confident the second round would go well—in fact cinch the deal—that it was more a matter of formalities and offer letters to sign so as to call the agency home. The interviews had become so cozy that one of the head creatives went as far as to show him the office he would be occupying. It was a match made in heaven. He had one interview left to do with the art director.

A week went by, and he didn't hear anything, so he decided to call. He left a message with reception to set up his third and final interview. Two days passed with no reply, so he sent an e-mail to the partner to see when he would have time to meet. Several painful days later he checked in to try to set an appointment.

He was being stonewalled—or so it seemed—locked out even though they showed him where he'd hang his shingle.

At best it was a rude way for the company to let him know his services would not be needed, *thank you very much*. At worst, in this market, with jobs at a minimum and interviews that went as well as his had gone, it was like someone jammed a burning stake right through his heart.

If this had been the fifteenth agency nonrejection rejection, it would have registered as a dark blip on the radar screen of control tower job search hell. But it was now a year into his search, a painful, slow, demoralizing, and fruitless search that felt like it would never pay off or ever end.

For him this was personal. More than a month had passed, and he knew at the time of the original meetings the agency was looking to make a hiring decision within a week after speaking with him. He told me all he could think and ask himself over and over in his head was, "what is wrong with me, what had they found on me that knocked me out of the running, is it my graying hair, is a former supervisor slandering me? They nearly hired me on the spot, showed me my office, and now I can't get them to acknowledge my existence," he whimpers over the phone.

He was starting to melt down. This was the interview, the company that was going to push him over the edge. He was devastated and needed help *now*.

"Dwain, I can't take it anymore," he huffs into the phone. I had never heard him speak like this as long as I had known him. It was alarming.

"Take what? Where are you?" I ask.

"It doesn't matter," he says. "I don't think I can take it. You've got to help me. You've got to drop everything and help. I don't care what you're doing or what's happening, I don't think I can go on!"

I leaned back in my chair, and I started asking him more questions. I am a journalist at heart and knew I needed more answers before I could offer any meaningful help. "Are you with anyone, are you outside, have you been drinking, taking drugs?" I ask him.

He said it didn't matter where he was and he hadn't been drinking. He wasn't slurring. I ask him again whether there was someone around besides me, three thousand miles across the country. He says he's alone. *That is bad.* I then ask him if he owed people money and it was time to pay up.

"That's none of your fucking business; I'm not going down that road with you," he blurts out.

He hung up on me.

I was surprised how quick to anger he became over that question. I thought the question was appropriate because one of my first thoughts was that maybe he owed someone money and they had come to collect.

I ran upstairs to tell my wife what was going on.

"Call his wife right now," Colleen says. "You need to let her know what's going on."

"I can't call her. He told me not to say anything to anyone. Besides, if I do let her know and it gets back to him he will never speak to me again. At least I have him talking this out with me."

"What are you talking about, can't you see he needs help?" my wife says in a more serious tone. "Call one of his friends out there then, maybe they know where he is. They're out there and they should know about it."

The phone rang and my friend's number illuminated my phone screen. I walked out of our bedroom and jogged back down two flights of stairs to the basement where I could talk in private and continue to freeze my nuts off. My kids were in bed. It was late here.

"Hi," I say. "You all right?"

"Sorry about that—sorry about hanging up on you. I shouldn't have done that, I'm really sorry," he says.

My mind was racing. I was trying to stay calm while at the same time trying to figure out what questions I could ask that wouldn't offend and yet give me a better picture of what was going on in his head.

He started sobbing.

I had never heard him cry before. I could feel his pain in ways he could never imagine.

It was difficult to listen to him bawl. It was probably the best thing he could do at this moment. It was keeping him alive. He needed to get this off his chest. I kept thinking how glad I was to be available for him and at the same time I couldn't help thinking how moments before he called me I had been sitting in my own dark place in my head. I was experiencing that which mirrored his world, right down to the thought of using a shotgun on myself. I shuddered at the absurdity of it all.

"I don't think I can recover this time," he says, when he could finally speak again. "I just don't think I can go on. I have *never* been this unhappy or so unfulfilled in my life. I can't see a reason for going on."

"Look, let's stay calm here. You can see I am calm, so you can stay calm with me. I don't know all that is going on where you are, but I do know we can figure this out together. Why don't I stay on the line and we conference in 911, and we will call for a ride to the hospital. There's nothing to be ashamed of. It's a stressful time and you need a break . . . to get back on your feet. They can give you some medicine that will help you settle down and get things back in perspective."

After a long pause he says, "Okay, I will call 911."

"Good, do you want me to stay on the line?"

"No, I'll call. You know, nobody cares about me anymore. I have nobody in my life and I can't get a real job. I'm sick of being unemployed."

And with that the phone went dead.

Ten minutes later he texts me: "I just want u 2 know that if we don't speak again I love you."

I immediately call him back. I go directly into voicemail.

I text him: "I just called you. Call me. You have options. You don't have to hurt urself tonight. I love you too."

At 3 a.m. my phone vibrated next to my bed with a message that said: "I'm ok. I'll talk to you tomorrow. Thx."

Tonight was rock bottom, I thought.

I lay in bed replaying the events in my head. How was it possible that two people living thousands of miles apart, with different careers, different emotional sensibilities, and completely different lifestyles, could be driven to their knees, harassed by demons that left us on the verge of catastrophic self-destruction as a result of spending less than a year out of full-time employment?

We were literally *letting* unemployment kill us.

It doesn't have to be this way, I told myself. I squeezed my eyes shut and as much as demanded it not be so. This doesn't have to destroy my life. For me, unemployment had become a life-threatening occupational hazard. For now, though, I told myself it does not exist when it is not happening and closed my eyes and fell back to sleep.

Avoiding the Comparison Trap

The longer I'm out of work, the more I find myself focusing on what everybody else around me has. Not just materialistically—sure I would like more money, at this point a steady stream in the form of a paycheck—to buy a bigger house, go on better vacations, or donate more to charity. Even when I had a job, I would catch myself comparing my lot in life. You know that feeling you get sometimes, that inferior feeling, but you don't know exactly why you're feeling that way? I've learned that comes about as a result of an unfavorable comparison to someone that took place either consciously or subconsciously in my mind. Comparing to others wreaks havoc on my self-confidence, it knocks me down, and I find myself swearing off it.

A therapist friend puts these feelings in perspective for me. "Do you know why confident people feel confident? Because they make favorable comparisons between them and other people. A confident person focuses on thinking about what is special about them, and if there is any comparing going on, they are comparing their attributes to ordinary people, and how special they are. Want to depress yourself? Spend the day comparing what you don't have to the rest of population where you live."

Comedian Susie Essman learned years ago how to keep grounded and not fall into the "grass is always greener" trap.

As I said, I just focus on the work and not the results, and I think it is a mistake to focus on what other people are doing. It's fine to be competitive with yourself, but, when you are constantly focusing on what other people are achieving, you get yourself in trouble. For example, I could be focused on comedians who are making lots more money than me, but it's a waste of time. Everybody has their own journey for lack of a better word. Everybody's marriage looks better than yours. Everybody has to go the way their own blood beats, and you have to be true to that. And, believe me, if I listened to practical people around me, I never would've had the career that I have today. I was told I will never make a living as a comedian.

I confess, the pain of being unemployed for all these months has made me look at money in a different way. I was deeply moved one day when I happened upon a video posted on my Facebook newsfeed entitled *What If Money Was No Object*, narrated by Alan Watts. Watts was a British-born philosopher, writer, and speaker who lived in the San Francisco Bay area, best known as an interpreter and advocate of Eastern philosophy for a Western audience. In the video Watts talks about doing what you want in life, about the advantages of a short life filled with things you love over a long life filled with the mundane and the pursuit of money for money's sake. What really surprised me was the narrative was set to a piece of music called *Divenire* by my favorite Italian pianist and composer, Ludovico Einaudi. I go back to this video from time to time, especially when I'm having a bad day. It's inspiring and beautiful to watch. The imagery is breathtaking in places, and the message reinforces that if you follow your dreams and pursue what you love, money will come—or at the very least most or all of your needs will be met and you will live a more blissful life.

I need to become more blissful and respect that landing a job takes the time that it takes. No sense adhering to an artificial deadline. Pamela Mitchell, CEO of the Reinvention Institute, reminds me that I control only what I put out there—and not what life brings back to me. So it doesn't pay to make myself crazy because I should be farther along in my search or whatever I'm trying to accomplish. She advises me to think about what I'm supposed to do every day and then let life handle its part. She doesn't need to remind me that it can take three weeks for a contact to get back to me.

Mitchell remembers having to surrender to the almighty timeline early on when she founded her company ten years ago. When she first started out, an entrepreneur friend told her it would take about five years for her business to gain traction, whereas she believed it would take two. Her friend was right! She learned to surrender, and that meant that she could spend more time building her marketing plan and getting the word out to a broader client base.

She counsels her clients who are looking to establish a new career path that the key to keeping your sanity while reinventing yourself is to embrace the journey as best you can and as often as possible. She says many people miss the gifts that are right in front of their noses when it comes to experiencing the journey and all that it has to teach you. She preaches that psychologically the journey is as important as the destination. Slow down and take pleasure in the learning, tap into the excitement of doing something new. The more you can let go of the job as the final "end," the more you'll realize that life is a series of continual new beginnings.

This sounds simple but it is not easy. There's a certain discipline that is required to shift how we think, but, again, we must keep in mind we are only partially in control of the process. She tells me a lot of men say to her that their ego has been damaged, and that's when she says to them that this is an opportunity to build their ego on a much stronger foundation. The breakthrough comes when a person knows that, no matter what happens, they can come out the other side on top.

> Most people are very self-motivated in this regard, so they think if they work harder, harder, and harder, they can somehow speed this up. But there are a lot of pieces that have to fall into place behind the scenes for your opportunity to show up, and you need to allow for that and go along for the ride to some degree.

When Friends Are Oblivious

Part of that journey is coming to terms with the obliviousness of the fully employed and financially secure—some of those being friends or family. Summer found me and my wife taking the kids to see their grandparents for vacation in Laguna Niguel, California. My parents live in what can simply be called paradise. Better yet, whenever we visit they generously pick up the tab. They belong to a luxurious beach club five miles from the house. Their back deck offers the sights that a soaring eagle can see—a panorama of the Pacific Ocean with Catalina Island to the north and San Clemente and Point Loma to the south.

When the kids aren't surfing at Doheny State Beach at Dana Point, they're swimming in the pool or playing with my parents' beloved golden retriever, Napa. It's a glorious place; I just wish I could enjoy it. The pressure of being unemployed never lets up. There is no average day being out of work. It is like putting on clothing that never comes off. It stays with you and melts into your skin, into your bloodstream. It's like being branded. There is no average day, and so it is in paradise I sit with this ball and chain called unemployment I dragged clear across the country, partially in hopes of shaking it loose for a week.

I got in touch with Rob, a friend I had gone to college with who was living in San Diego, seventy miles south of where we were staying. Rob owned a ski boat, and the plan was for me to take my three kids and join him and his two girls waterskiing for the day. I offered to bring hot dogs and hamburgers and other lunch stuff that we could cook on the boat. Rob owned several businesses and had done very well for himself, becoming a millionaire many times over since we went separate ways out of college. He lived a great life, and, unbelievable as it was to comprehend, his businesses continued to do well and grow in this terrible economy. As friends I shared with him early on about being let go and asked him on several occasions whether he had any openings at one of his companies. I laid out for him what I thought I could do for him and where he might be able to utilize my skills. Throughout the months there were several false starts, but nothing materialized. He didn't exactly say no to anything; he just never said yes. It was always this open-ended conversation that left me grasping for smoke rings in the end. I was careful not to put him on the spot or make him feel that I was somehow entitled because of our close friendship.

We packed my parent's Denali with beach towels and boogie boards and merged onto I-5 for the straight shot down the coast. It was a beautiful day, seventy-three degrees and sunny, just what you would expect for San Diego. San Diego doesn't have weather. It *experiences* climate. Think Mediterranean, and that's the kind of day we were having on the ocean, waterskiing, tubing, and fishing. The kids were having a blast getting reacquainted, and for a second I nearly pinched myself. I had set aside my feelings of inadequacy. Today wasn't about looking for a job or identifying myself as just another out-of-work schlub. I was living in the present, feeling the sea breeze on my face, tasting the salty air, smelling the boat motor exhaust. This was my journey today. It was fun catching up with my old college buddy too. We had quite a few laughs, and that reminded my why we had remained such good friends for so long.

I just wish I wasn't broke.

It was around 5 p.m. when the kids took their last ride on the oversized inner tube we dragged them around on in figure eights that day. They had hatched a plan for all of us to go out to dinner. I wasn't anticipating spending any money that evening. The fact that we were on vacation was bad enough on the checkbook (check that—credit card). The airline tickets alone cost $3,000 to get this far. I gave in, and off we went to a local Japanese restaurant. Anyone who has young kids appreciates their fascination with a hibachi chef preparing food over an iron tabletop grill right under their chins. It's a flamboyant show of flipping shrimp, spinning eggs, and the crowd favorite, flaming onion volcano. Throw in some knife juggling for good measure if the chef is adventurous.

The bill came and our portion added up to $125. I reached for my credit card and for a split second thought, *Rob is sure to offer to pick this one up.* It wasn't like I was asking him to subsidize me because my financial house of cards was about to collapse over a half-eaten plate of teriyaki steak and rice. This wasn't even a moral dilemma moment for me. He surely wouldn't think of me as a mooch who conveniently misplaced his wallet after a fun day at sea—Mr. Alligator arms who can't reach his pockets to cough up the cash? I had picked up plenty of restaurant tabs and forked over buckets of cash in my day to cover pub crawls over the years, especially in college.

The after-dinner banter had finally dwindled away, and it was time to pay up. He didn't say anything, and I cheerfully handed over my credit card. "We'll split it, sound good?" he asks. I said great, thanks.

As we left the restaurant the kids had decided they wanted dessert and eyeballed a frozen yogurt shop catty-corner to the restaurant. I pulled my middle daughter aside and said that I would rather pass. We've spent enough today—"pretty please, please . . . it will be fun," she says to me.

Rob is the first to order. The kids load up their self-serve cups with colorful flavors of the swirling frozen concoction and pile on the extras—Snickers crumbles, gummy bears, mini-chocolate chips, and an assortment of freshly cut berries. Life is good. While this is going on, I reach in my pocket and pull out a thin wad of crumpled bills. I start counting. I'd better be prepared to pay our share—without hesitation. I can hear my wife's voice in my head saying, "Don't use the credit card. Spend cash so when you run out for the month, that's all you can spend." Good advice, but I'm addicted to my credit card. Who isn't? It's free money . . . until the bill comes. These days I don't even open those bills. As far as I'm concerned, Citibank must have planted a tree in the corner of my backyard next to the lemon tree that transfers funds electronically to my account every month.

I think I have enough cash to cover the damage. *I won't need it, of course, this time.* I bring up the rear with my small dessert, and the cashier adds up the total. I look around and Rob is nowhere to be seen. Scratch that, he's outside with the kids. My son is also with them.

"That will be $41.67," the cashier says. I look around again. Nothing. It's just me, alone, and the cashier.

I fish out my credit card and hand it over.

I can't believe it. He knows I'm on the balls of my ass right now, and he's got more money than God.

I sign the receipt and join everyone outside. It's still seventy-three and sunny.

Standing under a canopy of palm trees lining the boulevard, everyone is enjoying their treats . . . except me. I look over at Rob finishing up his cone.

"Dude, thanks for the yogurt," he says to me. He looks over at his kids and says, "Guys, thank Mr. Schenck for the dessert."

In unison everyone says, "Thank you Mr. Schenck."

Another day in paradise.

9

REINVENTION—
IT'S YOUR TURN

Can You Pinpoint Opportunity?

I get it. Change is the new normal. With change comes new opportunities, new ideas, and out-of-the-ordinary experiences. Unemployment brings with it about as much change as a person could ask for . . . or want in two, maybe three lifetimes. And, with that change, my life got interesting . . . if you consider night sweats, depression, chronic worthlessness, and teetering on losing everything appealing.

My life has been hacked—I log on to find my entire existence redirected to a server selling extended release anti-inflammatories. Tap again and I'm on the Republic of Belarus tourism page, complete with red and green flag, music, and images of traditional cuisine—beetroot, bouillon, and river fish. Talk about time for a change.

If you live long enough and have the ability to step outside yourself once in a while, you realize that your problems are not unique—say, for example, from your neighbor's problems. As re-invention coach Pamela Mitchell likes to say, somewhere someone else had the same problem and figured out how to solve it success-fully. I relate more to how Brad Pitt's character Tyler Durden serves up reality in *Fight Club*: "You are not special. You're not a beautiful and unique snowflake. You're the same decaying organic matter as everything else. We're all part of the same compost heap."

Mitchell sees things through a rosier lens, thank God. She says that when we let go of the idea that we are the only person in the world who is facing a particular issue, we can begin to find solu-tions. "I say if you want bigger ponds to play in, you need to think about reinvention. That means thinking about yourself as a con-stellation of skills and talents and looking at multiple ways those skills and talents can be applied, whether it be within a corporate environment or for yourself. You need to shift into dealing with the new way the world operates today."

Are You Willing to Reinvent Yourself?

Wanting to reinvent yourself and being willing to reinvent your-self are two separate things. You must decouple the two and take action to accomplish your goals. As Mitchell tells me, there are always going to be aspects of your reinvention that you don't want to do—like taking a temp job to bring in cash for rent or picking up that five-hundred-pound phone to call a potential employer or networking contact.

"To reinvent yourself, you need to take a personal inventory, a survey of what your skills and talents are. Take yourself out of the job title box or the job function box and ask yourself, what skills do I use to perform those job functions? because those are the transferable skills," she says.

When I was let go, all I could do was think about how what I did *for a living* was the only thing I knew how to do. But I know other things. And because of that I went through my own reinvention of sorts and started writing this book. It's like bucking a society that keeps telling me I can only do one thing and specialize in one area, but I am learning that I'm more than that. I like the short phrase Mitchell uses, "constellation of skills." I do have some other interests even though I dismiss them as something that could never earn me a living wage. It's that kind of closed-minded thinking that would still have us riding horses to the store.

Clinical psychologist Dr. Barbara Lavi says that keeping your identity during challenging times like a recession of this magnitude has a lot to do with concentrating on feeling good about where you are and what you're doing in the here and now. Your dream should be to find peace with whatever it is you choose to do, whatever it is that makes your life feel meaningful. In essence, the meaning of life is to give life meaning, she says. And of course work gives many people meaning, but she emphasizes that work is only one part of the equation. Part of the challenge is to get away from the feeling that everything is happening *to* me and to take back control and make things happen *for* me.

Part of Dr. Lavi's therapy centers on helping clients reconnect with the creative side of their being in an effort to facilitate a successful reinvention. "One of the things I've been thinking about during this horrible downturn is the fear of change," Dr. Lavi says, as I sit across from her in her home office nestled in the woods of Weston, Connecticut.

I just did a whole lecture series about fear and how it can take our dreams hostage. Everybody has to find a way to dream, no matter what stage of life they are in. You have to find a way to dream so that you can imagine life will get better. So part of it is important to have the vision in order to start moving to something better. Dreaming is the catalyst to a better future, and, just as with every ending there is a beginning, in every beginning there is an end. And part of what makes endings so hard for us is that we are afraid of losing what we had—a job for example. Look what a tough time you're having.

Dr. Lavi's challenge for her patients and for those who buy her book *The Wake Up and Dream Challenge* is to come up with at least ten dreams that are more than just your job, or job related, but rather to include all of the parts of yourself that are important to represent. She stresses that this is also a technique that can allow you to "step outside of yourself and take back control. In psychology they call this the locus of control. When you lose your job, the locus of control typically feels like outside forces are controlling your existence. People typically see life as dictated by the outside world. The economy, everything that is going wrong, is perceived to be out of my control," she says. Dr. Lavi's dream exercises help to resist that feeling. It's better to believe that you have control, that you will make things happen regardless of the economy—and in fact things happen all the time that buck conventional wisdom. Just ask Microsoft, which was founded during a bruising recession, proving even in the worst of times there are opportunities lying in wait if you act upon them.

Dreaming will give your life more fullness and make you realize that *you* are more than just a job. It will help you find your way out of the abyss, out of the darkness. I have used this to help people reawaken their spirit, and part of it is letting go of the fantasy that they may have had before something bad happened. They don't have to buy into the idea that they are going to be stuck in some bad situation for the rest of their life.

When it comes to dreaming, few dream bigger than Donald Trump. He has taken Macy's by storm with his line of clothing and housewares, and his TV reality show *The Apprentice* and its incarnations are still a ratings bonanza for NBC. He is a master at the art of reinvention and transformation, and as such he tells me that, when it comes to choosing a new career, people don't always take what he's about to say seriously enough when they consider making a change:

I think more than anything else you have to love what you're doing. That keeps you sharp. If you like what you're doing, you will tend to do it well, but you have to love what you do. I tell people all the time don't take the job unless you're going to love it. Otherwise it's just not going to work out.

What he says profoundly applies to me. As badly as I want to get back in the workforce, I have reluctantly and to my detriment dragged my feet on interviewing with public relations agencies. Although I have the skills to work at a PR agency and I ran my own agency for eleven years, I prefer the corporate side of communications, and my goal is to get back to heading up communications for a growing midsize company that is doing exciting work in technology or an exciting start-up that is big enough to bring on somebody at my level.

How High Can You Jump?

Beggars can't be choosers in this marketplace, though. You have to jump at anything that comes up. Remember what Mika said. Deloitte LLP CEO Joe Echevarria suggested that it may take going way out on a limb to get to where you want to be:

> Sometimes I advise people when they are trying to reinvent themselves to do something for free. If someone came into my office and they had all these great skills and they say, "I don't know if you need these great skills or not but I will just do some things around here on my nickel"—I'm being extreme here to make a point—but perhaps they can find a way to add value that I would change my lens and say maybe I didn't need that skill but I needed that personality and I needed that attitude and I need somebody who was willing to do something to prove to me their value.

I ask Echevarria whether he needs some light filing or perhaps a press release written, anything—for free, of course.

> I like people who hustle. I came from an environment where we had to hustle to survive, so I like people who are willing to hustle for me or for the enterprise or for the people I serve. There are never enough of those people around—EVER. You

have to be willing to do some things that you never were willing to do before. If I lost my job tomorrow, I would go out and hustle. I like to teach, so I would go to a university and say, "I'll teach for free, I'll teach the one thing no one wants to do on this campus, and I'll do it for nothing, and if I am really good, someone will find room for me."

Mika agrees. She says job seekers need to think about freelancing to pave the way for their next full-time gig:

I took a freelance position for much lower pay when I went back to work. But you know what the freelance position allows you to do? It allows you to prove your worth. I would almost offer to work freelance if the full-time deal you're being offered isn't good. Knowing what you're worth is all about reinventing yourself. If you know you're worth more than you're being offered, but you need the job, you've got to be so self-aware about what you can bring to the table for the company. You need to know that you can go in and blow their socks off with the work you do. Work freelance for a while and regroup, give them way more than they're paying for, stay loose so that you can nail them six months later for a full-time job at full scale.

Contracting also helped Peter Propp rejuvenate his career. Propp was the original business development manager for IBM's WebSphere product family, now a multibillion-dollar business that supports the web business integration efforts for many of the world's most sophisticated web applications. Propp left IBM to start his own marketing strategy and consulting business, where he worked for hundreds of small technology companies and start-ups before taking his current title of vice president of marketing for the Stamford Innovation Center in Connecticut. The center is an incubator for high-tech start-ups, offering coworking space, educational programming, and accelerator programs that drive collaboration among entrepreneurs, investors, and industry experts. I visited the location. It gives new meaning to the word *reinvention*. Before becoming part of the organization's management team, Propp took on several freelance projects, one of which was doing the marketing for an event called Stamford Startup Weekend. He sold it out.

In the spirit of inventing a business from scratch, entrepreneur attendees spent the first part of the weekend pitching their ideas to the entire group, which voted for the most promising ten ideas. The participants then divided up into small teams and spent the rest of the weekend focusing on a single business idea. Over the course of the weekend, they built a fully functioning start-up, including developing a business model, proof of concept, and basic prototype. Local business leaders then joined in the fun, offering one-on-one advice to each team. The weekend concluded on Sunday evening, when teams pitched their concepts to a panel of potential investors and local entrepreneurs. According to Propp:

> Programs like Startup Weekend are powerful because they provide real-life experiences to would-be entrepreneurs. We are working hard to teach these entrepreneurial skills and bring young people and experienced executives up to speed with programs like this. We teach people new skills and approaches to problems. I am a big believer that we need to help people coming out of the corporate landscape develop

the skills that are going to be helpful if they want to create a start-up. We hope a lot of them come take us up on the offer, because start-ups generate a lot of jobs. There is more job creation happening right now at start-ups than anywhere else. Corporations are forever worrying about delivering increased returns to shareholders, and that can mean reducing their head count all the time. We're a catalyst for generating scalable new business ideas and, ideally, good-paying jobs.

Can You Pinpoint Opportunity?

As I look around, I can see all kinds of exciting things are happening. People are reinventing things and reinventing themselves in this economy in ways they would have never dreamed of doing before the crash. And that's the point. One good thing that is coming out of this crisis is that it is forcing individuals to take chances and risk failure to do something new. I would bet that, when historians look back on this window in time, more entrepreneurs and entrepreneurial endeavors will have been launched than any time in modern history.

The way we get our food and what we eat is a good example. No need to leave the city to be on the farm. Along with the moniker concrete jungle, New York City and some of the outer boroughs can now add another nickname to the list, Green Acres, USA. Rooftop commercial agriculture or urban farming, spurred on by a down economy, has taken a foothold in Manhattan, which has become a leader in the urban farming movement. At the rate our population is growing, some scientists believe that in the next thirty years vertical farming, many stories high, situated in the heart of cities, will solve the problem of producing a safe, cost-effective, year-round crop of varied foods—augmenting the horizontal farms that we rely on to feed our hungry nation today.

Other amazing things are happening in the great big national picture. Enterprises like IBM, Eli Lilly, Coca Cola, and other large multinational corporations are sitting on trillions of dollars, and estimates show that approximately ten thousand baby boomers are retiring every day. What does that mean? We have all been wringing our hands in America over the fiscal cliff, the sequester, and the recession—rightly so—but are any of us thinking that THIS isn't going to last forever? Recessions come and go, thank God. It may be too soon to say this—but are we going to have the right people to fill all of these jobs that are being vacated by all of these boomers?

Can You Think Counterintuitively About the Market?

Founder of Jobs4.0 and host of CBS radio's *Your Next Job* Steven Greenberg says corporate America is oblivious to the labor challenges ahead of them.

Greenberg recently commissioned the first-ever survey to determine the best employers in the United States for job seekers over forty. Employers were judged on more than twenty separate criteria, including rates of new hires of workers over forty, recruitment policies and goals, health benefits and job security for older workers, flexible work options for older workers, and more. "This is the first time any survey has tried to capture this essential data," Greenberg said.

"What we found is there is a tidal change coming in labor demographics that will hit corporate America like a tsunami. In the coming years over seventy-six million baby boomers will retire, but only forty-six million younger workers are in line to replace them. The median age of the US workforce will soon be over forty, for the first time in many generations." Greenberg says that, although his company, Jobs4.0, a job board that caters to job seekers forty and above, talks to major employers all over the United States and can report that some are already planning for these changes, far too many are out of step with what is coming down the pike.

> The survey identifies some of the most forward-thinking employers. These employers are already taking steps to attract a segment of the labor pool that has been ignored by major employers for too long.
>
> The survey results are also a unique and valuable resource for job seekers over forty. Older job seekers desperately want to find employers who will not view their age and experience as something to be avoided. Ageism in hiring remains prevalent in too many places, and this survey helps point older job seekers—not only retiring baby boomers, but all workers forty and above—in the right direction.

There is also a crisis in the world of academia. Tenured professors are retiring in numbers that can't be replaced. There are so few professors on the tenure track that the regents of the University of California have taken up the issue to see what can be done to fill the ranks. These shortages are happening everywhere just under the radar at the moment, and that creates huge opportunity. "There are always jobs out there. There just are," says Donny Deutsch, with his signature enthusiasm. "You have to be creative. There are always businesses doing well, looking for bright people who bring value to the bottom line who can help them do better."

Social media marketing expert Beverly Macy tells her students to start thinking more counterintuitively about the marketplace. Companies also need to start thinking smarter about how they go about hiring and nurturing employees. There is a significant investment made by employers to bring on employees to then just go through mass layoffs every time the business cycle turns.

"It takes nearly eighteen months to two years to function fully within an organization," says Pamela Mitchell. "That's when you're integrated and everybody knows who you are, they know what to expect from you, you've got a track record, you've got all the knowledge you need, and the relationships have come together within the organization for you to be a valuable team member."

She indicates that companies can be more competitive and reinvent themselves by breaking out of the mold of looking at their key staffers as core experts, that is, marketing, finance, PR experts, and instead looking at the skills and talents their employees have. They need to ask themselves, "Okay, we've invested in this person; where else can we use them?" Because the old method of hire and fire and mass layoffs is costly on many levels and can set a company back light-years in the age of our knowledge economy. Mitchell suggests companies look at how to use people they have and figure out ways to move them into new markets so as not to lose momentum. Many companies are still using the business model of incorporating mass layoffs as a workforce reallocation tool.

Danger Will Robinson, danger! Like the robot seeing danger signs in *Lost in Space*, companies have to also add a little more emotion and intuition to their calculus when making decisions, as technology has changed so rapidly that they are starting to find they can no longer dump staff members and then go hire new talent and expect to be competitive. Today three years is pretty much like a midterm business plan, Mitchell says, and looking out any further is like throwing a dart at the wall:

> You can't really say in five to seven years where you'll be. You can make assumptions as to where you would like your business to be, but the truth is it can completely change, as evidenced by just looking at the cellular market landscape. Look at where BlackBerry was five years ago versus Apple and the iPhone. BlackBerry laid off one-third of its employees. Five years ago they were on top. And, as you know, it takes a good year to be integrated politically within a company. In that year of integration, the marketplace will have shifted again.

Macy is optimistic about the future growth of the economy, though she warns growth won't necessarily come in the form of traditional mass hirings, where, for example, five thousand people are brought on at a factory that just opened down the street.

—————

Okay, but we have to deal with the real world today, and although people I respect are seeing a more hopeful future, how does that affect me? "Think of the letter U. We're at the top on the left-hand side, and life is good, and everything is happening in your favor, but then we start sinking and sinking. We get laid off, and the economy sucks, and we keep sinking, and nobody can find work, and unemployment has run out, and the government can't figure things out," Macy says, attempting to answer my question or at least further explain where we still are. All I know is I'm at the bottom of the U and I'm drowning down there—somebody help me!

Eventually you have to come up on the other side of the U, and I think a lot of people are in the process of looking at this and saying, "Wow, I'm in a crisis and this isn't changing next Monday." If we looked at this in medical terms, we would say this patient is in critical care. Some of us are barely on life support and have to stop the bleeding. But—and it's an important *but*—it's beginning to change. We are starting to see daylight and that is exciting stuff.

Without hesitation she insists that, by the time this book hits the stores, certain industries will be experiencing a shortage of workers to fill key positions—"People will need to get educated for this new economy because in some cases companies will be in a hiring frenzy, especially in the STEM disciplines. The fiscal cliff will be ancient history, and much of the market problems are going to get resolved, one way or another. Corporations are sitting on so much money that merger and acquisition activity will also start going through the roof again."

She has a point. If you look abroad, emerging markets like India, China, Brazil, and Russia are already starting to take off. A rising middle class is churning out millions of new consumers who are snapping up more iPhones, Buicks (in China's case), and real estate.

We're all in the knowledge business now, and companies and workers are scrambling to learn what that is and how to exploit it. New technology and methods to harness the power of computing are also fueling innovation and growth. Science, medicine, education, even private space travel—brought to you from the rocket scientists at SpaceX in Southern California—are helping to rejuvenate the aerospace industry and are becoming the leading nontraditional launch provider for NASA. This is a very "disruptive" way of doing business, where the agency is committing billions of dollars to help private companies like SpaceX become a big part of the answer to the question of what will follow the space shuttle.

It's also boom time for alternative fuel entrepreneurs. Look at what's going on in North Dakota. The state's unemployment rate hovers around 3 percent (as of this writing), the lowest in the country, as its population continues to surge as a result of the oil industry jobs that have made the Rough Rider state the second-largest producer of crude behind Texas. With booms like that come hundreds of other jobs to support the industry. Did you miss the story about McDonalds paying $300 signing bonuses and hourly wages of up to $18 to serve hamburgers to the influx of truck drivers, frack hands, pipe fitters, teachers, doctors, and strippers?

Don't worry; you don't have to take up living in a little house on the prairie, minus thirty degrees Fahrenheit to start over. Whether we are conscious about it, many of us are taking steps every day at re-inventing ourselves right where we are. People are deciding, "maybe I don't want to go back to work for a big pharmaceutical company where I had a career for twenty years." Maybe it's time to . . . fill in the blank. Start a business. Downsize. Retire. People are starting to do amazing things. Things they never thought they would be doing, but out of necessity they're branching out and creating a new life.

Yes, Veronica, There Is a Silver Lining to All This

As devastating as job loss can be, Dr. Lavi says that for some people the experience comes with a silver lining.

It is never easy to come to terms with something as serious as dedicating your whole life to a career and then waking up one morning and it is gone. On the other hand, I work with clients who learn to see this as a once-in-a-lifetime opportunity to be home. There's a mix here, and it's more likely that a woman who has lost her job will say, "Oh, I felt like I had to work, and I left my children at home, and now I'll be home for them."

Even if this is a temporary condition, for some women it is a revelation, offering them a new perspective on their life. I help them understand what a nice side benefit to losing a job can be. For men, many don't see it that way. But I do see that changing.

I ask her, what about people who want to go back into their field? They loved doing what they did, marketing or whatever, and they want to stay at it. "They need to keep networking and telling themselves that they are going to get a job, because that's what they want and they have positioned their dream that way," Dr. Lavi says. I tell her I'm the guy who just keeps putting one foot in front of the other.

From the outside looking in, from the inside looking out, the more insight I have received through my own journey in writing this book, I start to realize that old friends and new friends I've picked up along the way, stretching from Hollywood to Midtown Manhattan and points north and south, have helped build my confidence. They have helped me become a stronger, better, more educated job seeker. I dream more since meeting Dr. Lavi, and that helps me get through my own job-loss blues.

As some of these folks so painfully pointed out early in my journey, there is nervousness in the voice of an unemployed person, which can be very exhausting. Were they talking about me? I wonder. As one high-profile celebrity who shall go unnamed said to me, "It's like the person wants to eat you up because they're so desperate for a job. They have to work on that." The critique continues: "There is this kind of tense neediness that is destructive because it's going to change the outcome of the meeting, interview, or phone call for the worse. It's almost a hysteria in your voice that only makes people tired of talking with you, and that's the tough talk that unemployed people need to hear." Thanks for the advice, I say. *Maybe next time you could not sugar coat it so much.*

I get it—this person was doing me a favor when I was starting out. Most employed people are afraid to say stuff like that to people like us because they don't want to destroy any hope we might have left to keep on keeping on. It's this kind of tough love that has helped me. I'm getting more callbacks. I'm doing better on interviews. I'm taking control of the conversation when it's appropriate, asking smart questions, staying on point. I'm getting closer to landing a job. I can feel it. Whether he realized it, when Donny Deutsch said jumping back into a corporate career is ancient history after fifty, my heart sank, and I tucked my tail for the rest of the day. He also did me a huge favor. You see, he can get away with saying that because he is not emotionally attached to my success or the marketplace. He speaks reality for anyone who wants to listen. It's up to me to decide whether to accept the truth or continue to live in denial. He also preaches the importance of taking risks. He's living proof you're never too young or too old to risk starting a new career or building a new and exciting future:

For me, I keep regenerating my life. I had children later—two little kids. I've challenged myself to start a new career. I've built a very successful advertising agency but I sold it, forcing myself into a new challenge, which is television. I'm not at the top of the heap yet, and that keeps me going. And trying to stay as young and fit as I can is important. Not to look young; I never tell people to dye their hair or anything like that, but constantly challenging myself gives me a certain energy, a certain vitality that is essential to my life.

Mika's Second Act

Mika's path to her next act after being fired from CBS is a textbook example of how one should reimagine a new beginning in this economy. She knows what it's like to walk out that door. No cell phone. No security badge (just like me at the beginning of this story). No e-mail address. She also knows what it takes to commit yourself to picking up the pieces when you feel "washed up and losing your looks." Here is more about Mika's invaluable experience on how to beat the job-loss blues and get yourself back in the game, in her own words:

> When I was fired I fell right to the very bottom. It was epic. I had that "who am I" moment. I was forty, a woman, and I was on TV. As you know, television is a very unforgiving business. You either have to be the five established women—Barbara Walters, Katie Couric, Diane Sawyer, and a few others—and then you've got all the young skinny lip-glossed supermodels who think they're going to last forever, and they flame out. I was right in the middle of that. I felt I had nothing. Honestly,

when Joe Scarborough decided to choose me as his cohost, I felt he was the only person on the face of the earth who saw what I knew and what I had to offer and that somewhere in me there was something so relatable and so much more valuable than some skinny FOX chick. Why? Because I was real. But as great as that was I still remember looking at him and couldn't imagine working those early-morning hours. The other thought that crossed my mind was I wondered why Joe would want to hire a washed-up housewife who had been fired from network television. "That's exactly why I want to hire you. *You* are real," he said to me. "You've seen a little something, you've been around the block, you've been churned out of the business just like I was churned out of politics. *We have something to offer* because we've been around and we've lived to tell about it."

You know what, I sat down on the set, and I was, for the first time ever in my career in television, myself. And you know what? Me being myself sold better than I ever did imitating other people in my other career lifetime.

In the beginning I had so many bad interviews. I remember one interview with CNN where I was so terrible I felt like yelling out, "I can't take it, I'm a loser!" Within a few months of being let go, money worries started to dog me. I felt the pressure of not getting interviews, the fear of rejection when I did get an interview, and, when I wasn't out meeting people to find a job, I wallowed in sadness and loneliness. I explain it probably best in my memoir, *All Things at Once*, what I felt like in an interview. I wore my "fired" label on my forehead.

I went to FOX. It was bad. FOX didn't want me. When I say bad, I mean when I went to the interview I tried to "look" and "be" really "hot." Oh God, I looked like a clown. I wasn't hot. I wasn't even close. It was a painful, desperate attempt to get back in the business and give them what I thought they wanted. I honestly looked like Tammy Faye Bakker or some kind of wannabe beauty queen.

When I finally went back to work at MSNBC, I was done with all of that. I was like, screw it! I'm going to go in and wear jeans, and I'm going to do these news cut-ins (short news headlines inserted into a broadcast), and I'm going to go home. I'm starting at the very bottom, and I'm going to work nights again, but I'm not going to stress myself out. This is who I am, this is where I am, stop thinking I can be something that I am not. I'm not that anymore, this is where I am.

I had truly let go. Being told to be yourself is one of the most frustrating pieces of advice to hear because who are you when you don't know who you are? And with that, how do you be yourself?

Let go is what I did, and who I was started to bubble to the surface. I advise you too to let go of what you had in your career because it's gone. Now, what can you do? What is available to you? Do it, do it. That's what I did. I took a job that fifteen years ago was way beneath me. That is a dangerous attitude to have, though. I went from being a *60 Minutes* correspondent to odd man out. What I had was better than nothing, and I was damned grateful. I cleaned the garbage in my office at MSNBC. I organized my clothes and was on my hands and knees organizing my shoes and Joe's shoes, which were in the closet next to mine, because they were a mess. When I was through being the shoe lady, I went outside and organized the news schedule with the scheduler. Then I carried a huge box of coats downstairs that were supposed to be taken down by someone else. The point is, I'm above nothing and so glad to be doing it. How I got here was to be above nothing. To be above nothing and get back in was my life's mission. I literally said I will clean the garbage. In return just give me a job.

I realize now I was reinventing myself in a way that I didn't know I was doing it. That's why today I say sometimes the best reinventions are unexpected. I had planned reinventions and coordinated them, like when I went from CBS overnights to MSNBC homepage. They gave me a total makeover, and they bought me clothes and chopped off my hair—another Tammy Faye Baker moment—trying to fashion me into a beauty queen. It didn't work. It was other people trying to make me into something that I wasn't. It also turned out to be the most expensive, planned-out reinvention I ever had. It failed because it was forced.

There's a thing about just letting it happen that I've learned about life. I am pretty type A and controlling. I'm super controlling actually; I'm a working mom and I write everything out. I have a lot of people in my life I am coordinating with, but usually I'm controlling things; I am decisive, organized, and keep lists at work. That personality trait doesn't mix well in the case of dealing with the emotional side of being unemployed. You've got to let go, have some trust, be confident in who you are, know who you are, and find out what you're made of as things happen. You can't get in the way of that, and I find unemployed people like me when I was unemployed, are so hyperfocused on trying to get one thing back that they miss all these other things they could have gotten if they were emotionally open in a Zen or meditative sort of way. That is not normal for people like me and you. So, you have to constantly fight it and center yourself.

In this economy you have to take whatever job you can get. I would spend six months thinking I was going to get something that was just not happening. My agent was telling me, "You can still get this, but you know what, you have to think for yourself, and you have to think realistically and think small and hope that you will be pleasantly surprised." You are starting all over again and that's just the way it goes in this market . . . and that's okay.

10

LOST AND FOUND

What I've Learned

Here's what I've learned. I've learned to ask a lot of questions. Asking questions is the lifeblood of landing a job. That's what I've learned. Here's what I mean.

People are willing to help you all day long, but if you don't ask them for their help—and more importantly explain in detail how they can help—you will be lost in space without a jetpack. I have been asking for a lot of help these many handfuls of months. I've also been conscious of the fact that the people I admire most who have jobs show gratitude I haven't seen in the past decade when it comes to employment.

I truly understand what Joe Scarborough means when he says he feels guilty even thinking about complaining about the ups and downs of his job or the unbearable hours he and Mika put in these days. They make it look fun and easy, but it's not. It's hard work, but like his father before him he learned at a young age to be grateful for the job he has and to be working and providing for his family.

I think we can all learn from the wisdom he has attained as a US representative for the state of Florida right down to being a coach for his boy's Little League baseball team: "It's incredibly important to be optimistic and play to your strengths, waking up in the morning knowing that something good is going to happen," Scarborough tells me on the phone as he and Mika race across town to an event in Manhattan. "What happens to me is, when something good doesn't happen, I get angry, and I wake up the next morning even more driven, and I keep going like that every day."

It is that optimism and vision that helped him start a whole new career after spending six years in Congress.

On the very day I left office, the local paper asked me, "What are you going to do next?" I said I'm going to practice law and then get a TV show! Everybody laughed at me. I remember Jeb Bush a year later asking me, "So, where's that TV show, Congressman Joe?" I knew I was going to do that. You talk about reinvention—I had just decided that was what I was going to do, and I made phone calls and pushed and pulled, and I received a lot of push back from networks, but I kept going, and by the end of 2002 they called me up and said come on over. Let's talk.

It has required a lot of sacrifice for Scarborough and his family to get to where he is today, but he is quick to say it turned out to be as happy of an ending as he could have ever imagined. I remind him that he is far from the end.

And, as fate would have it, a new beginning was starting to take shape for me. While all of this time I was interviewing for full-time positions, I started to pick up more and more small freelance PR consulting and writing jobs along the way, especially as I am coming to a close in writing this book. A friend of mine hired me to do some writing for his website, and that led to some work writing corporate bios for another friend's website.

I had also been nurturing a relationship to do executive communications work for a managing director of a media and information company that was starting to materialize in New York City.

Then my wife brought to my attention a writing opportunity at a local nonprofit organization. I was familiar with the organization and believed that I could do more for them than writing if they had any marketing or PR positions open. I e-mailed my résumé to the recruiter and called to see whether I could set up an interview.

I was put in touch with human resources, who set up a meeting the next day. Things were moving quickly. It was unsettling, actually, how quickly things were taking shape. Within a week I was sitting in front of the CEO interviewing for a communications position. The meeting went great, and I thought there was a good chance I might finally land the full-time job I've been looking for all this time.

The following weekend the CEO called me while I was watching my daughter play softball to see if I might consider joining her organization on a temporary basis—sort of a try-before-you-buy arrangement. I said yes. This would be a great addition to the portfolio of clients I already had.

Without consciously planning it, but certainly working it every step of the way for the past year and a half, my own reinvention was finally blossoming. I had finally let go and gone with the constellation of talent theory my friend Pamela Mitchell had so eloquently talked about. I also had embraced what Mika had been saying all along: Snatch up the first freelance opportunity that comes my way. Chances are it will turn into the full-time job of my dreams, or at the very least keep the wolves away from the door for another week.

The handful of consulting jobs I now have has allowed me to incorporate under the name Schenck Strategies LLC (www .schenckstrategies.com). I've even hired other professionals to help me with the workload. In many respects I'm back to doing what I did before the Great Recession but at a much higher level, having a lot more fun and making more money.

I am grateful to my new clients for the confidence they have shown me. What many of them may not know is how much harder I work on their behalf because I never want to be unemployed again. It's a win-win. My clients are made up of influential individuals, corporations, and organizations in media, finance, entertainment, politics, and philanthropy. My small firm provides a broad range of high-level communications services including strategic counsel, corporate positioning, profile management, message development, media relations, brand building, and crisis management.

This journey has not been easy. That's an understatement if you're still with me here. Conversely, it has forced me to step outside of myself and be as honest as possible in hopes that I can help thousands of people like you reading this book take heart that you're not alone in your own struggles to land on your feet, whether it be in a new job or a reinvented life. We all eventually find our path to salvation, and no two people are alike or experience that journey the same way.

This book may be coming to a close, but our conversation together is just beginning if you like. I will continue to share what I've learned and speak to anyone who will listen or who is interested in learning how to keep their sanity and their identity while preparing for their next, greatest act—landing a new job!

I say be with it—whatever it is—right now. Be open and kind and do your work, and be grateful, because even if you're sick and they chop off your legs and they don't return your calls, you have a hell of a lot to be grateful for. You don't need a guru; you don't need a special prayer; you don't need to emulate anyone. . . . You have the strength. You have the power. You can do a lot of shit. Do the shit.

—Susan Tyrrell, 1942–2012, actress
James Grissom's blog post, June 18, 2012

INDEX

on job search timeline, 63

on networking, 83, 86, 97

on online job search diagnostics program, 65–67, 143

on "supreme confidence shield," 142–143

Suicide rate, xxii

"Supreme confidence shield," 142–143

Technology, 22–23, 206–107

The Ten Laws of Career Reinvention (Mitchell), 23

TheLadders (online job board), 60

Therapy, 107. *See also* Mental health, and
    unemployment

Thompson, Teri, 48

Tofel, Cliff, 106

Tosh.O (TV series), 11

Transferable skills, 79, 195

Trump, Donald, xxiii, 117, 131, 197

Tumblr, 57

Tweeting/Twitter, 49, 50, 53, 54, 57

Tyrrell, Susan, 219

Tyson, Mike, 61

UCLA, 50, 57

Unemployment

    and age discrimination, 115–119

    and buyers' market, 104–119

    and change, 193, 195–196 (*see also* Career
       reinvention)

    and comparisons, favorable and unfavorable, 184